OPPORTUNITIES

SO-BEH-744

in

Physician
Careers

OPPORTUNITIES

in

Physician Careers

REVISED EDITION

JAN SUGAR-WEBB

McGraw·Hill

New York   Chicago   San Francisco   Lisbon   London   Madrid   Mexico City
Milan   New Delhi   San Juan   Seoul   Singapore   Sydney   Toronto

Library of Congress Cataloging-in-Publication Data

Sugar-Webb, Jan, 1954–
    Opportunities in physician careers / Jan Sugar-Webb.— Rev. ed.
        p.   cm.
    ISBN 0-07-143848-3
    1. Medicine—Vocational guidance.   I. Title.

    R690.S84   2005
    610.69—dc22   2004017967

1 2 3 4 5 6 7 8 9 0   DOC/DOC   0 9 8 7 6 5

ISBN 0-07-143848-3

Interior design by Rattray Design

Contents

PREFACE

THE DECISION TO enter the medical profession is an important and life-changing event. Many people choose to study and practice medicine because they are drawn to the excitement and challenges that come with being a doctor. They thrive on the high-pressure work, where life and death decisions must sometimes be made in a matter of minutes. They also welcome the intellectual, physical, and emotional challenges of a demanding job. For many future physicians, the decision to pursue this career is motivated by a calling to work in a field that really makes a difference in people's lives, where the rewards of helping others by relieving their pain and suffering is even more important than the excellent salary opportunities and prestige associated with being a doctor.

Now more than ever, those drawn to a career in medicine face an astonishing array of possibilities. Medical students can choose from dozens of medical specialties and subspecialties and a wide range of environments. They may elect to work in hospitals, research laboratories, private practice, or overseas with underprivileged populations. They may focus specifically on helping children, women, the aged, or populations here and abroad affected by AIDS and other medical crises.

Whatever area of medicine you choose, you can be assured that this field will demand your best. The grueling medical school preparation, followed by intensive hands-on residency training, will test your limits and strengthen your character. Medicine is truly a field that calls for the best and brightest of our population. The challenges facing the medical profession are numerous; the need for qualified, caring physicians is constant; and the opportunities for a fulfilling career are there for all.

1

Physicians: A Historical Perspective

Throughout human history, people in need have turned to special practitioners who know how to relieve pain and suffering. From the earliest spiritual healers to today's experts in the latest medical techniques, the history of medicine reflects the integral role played by health practitioners.

Our ancient ancestors believed that evil spirits were the cause of disease and death. In the cosmic view of primitive peoples, a web of mystical processes was responsible for natural occurrences. These early humans believed, for example, that rain and fertility were all dependent on the goodwill of unseen gods and spirits. Illness was thought to arise when a spirit invaded the body. Health could be obtained only by following the whims and rules of these spirits. For that reason, the earliest "doctors" were considered sorcerers, people who could communicate with and ward off malevolent spirits.

At the Cave of the Three Brothers in France, explorers found what is likely the oldest picture of a healer. In the painting, done on a wall in the cave perhaps 25,000 years ago, a figure is dancing; he has human feet but the paws of a bear, and antlers sprout out of his head. It is believed that this person is a tribal doctor, wrapped in animal skins and driving evil spirits away. His ability to do magic gave him the power to heal the sick.

Ancient Egyptians

Archaeologists working at ancient sites of human habitation have found evidence that our ancestors used herbal therapies and even primitive surgery to heal the sick. Perhaps the most skillful and advanced medical practices of the ancient world could be found in Egypt.

Ancient Egyptians believed in immortality and that the soul would return to the body sometime after death. Egyptians preserved the bodies of the dead along with treasured possessions. They documented events on writing material called papyrus. The medical papyri of Egyptian physicians describe the ways they treated ailments and reveal a detailed knowledge of anatomy.

Although the Egyptians had a relatively advanced understanding of the human body, their medical practices still involved magic. They believed that many diseases were caused by wormlike creatures that invaded the body. Physicians and magicians would work together, combining medicines and spells to treat everything from scorpion stings to broken bones.

The most famous and detailed medical papyri are named after the men who obtained them in Egypt and shared them with the world—Smith and Ebers. The Smith papyrus outlines 48 surgical cases, including diagnoses and methods of treatment. It deals exclusively with wounds and fractures. The treatment offered for the cases is mostly practical but suggests a mix of magical incantations and remedies, including one "to change an old man into a youth of 20."

The Smith papyrus is an impressive document. The author of the original papyrus was probably a gifted surgeon who used practical interventions, like the following recommendation for treating a fractured collarbone:

> You must lay him down outstretched on his back, with something folded between his two shoulder blades. Then you must spread his two shoulder blades so that his two collarbones stretch, so that the fracture falls into its proper place. Then you must make him two compresses of cloth. Then you must place one of them inside his upper arm, the other below his upper arm . . .

Some of the recommended treatments are still used today. When the ailing patient has a dislocated jaw, the doctor is instructed to put his or her thumbs inside the patient's mouth. The doctor's other fingers go under the patient's chin, and the doctor guides the jaw back into its proper place. This manipulation is still the only treatment for a dislocated jaw.

The Ebers papyrus, which was probably composed around 2000 B.C., is mostly a text on internal medicine. It names diseases and remedies as well as some cosmetic aids. Like the Smith papyrus, parts of the Ebers papyrus contain observant medical data:

> If you examine a person who suffers from pains in the stomach and is sick in the arm, the breast, and the stomach, and it appears that it is the disease *uat*, you will say: "Death has entered into the mouth and has taken its seat there." You will prepare a remedy composed of the following plants: the stalks of the plant *tehus*, mint, the red seeds of the plant *sechet*; and you will have them cooked in beer; you will give it to the sick person and his arm will

be easily extended without pain, and then you will say, "The disease has gone out from the intestine through the anus, it is not necessary to repeat the medicine."

The Ebers papyrus also contains more magical treatments for diseases, like a frog warmed in oil for a burn. (This treatment is to be accompanied by a chant.)

Hippocrates and the Influence of Greek Medicine

Although contributions to medicine came from many eras in history and many places in the world, the Greeks have had the greatest influence on modern Western medicine. Nowhere in Homer's *Iliad*, written between 900 and 800 B.C., does he mention any incantations to treat the wounds of war. Instead, Homer writes of treatments that were strictly medical.

The most famous of the Greek physicians was Hippocrates, who is known as the "father of medicine." Hippocrates was born around 460 B.C. on the island of Cos, where he founded a school of medicine. His teachings, which included careful, detailed observation of the patient, encouraged the separation of medicine and religion and gave a scientific and moral basis to medicine. Hippocrates wrote:

> In acute diseases the physician must make his observations in the following way. He must first look at the face of the patient and see whether it is like that of people in good health, and, particularly, whether it is like its usual self, for this is the best of all; whereas the most opposite to it is the worst, such as the following: nose sharp, eyes hollow, temples sunken, ears cold and contracted and their lobes turned out, and the skin about the face dry, tense, and parched, the color of the face as a whole being yellow or black, livid or lead colored . . .

Hippocrates also taught that wounds should be washed in boiled water and that doctors' hands should be clean. Many of the observations that Hippocrates and his pupils made about the human body are still valid in terms of modern Western medicine. Some of these include:

- When sleep puts an end to delirium it is a good sign.
- Weariness without cause indicates disease.
- If there be a painful affection in any part of the body, but no suffering, there is mental disorder.

Hippocrates also had a moral vision of what a physician should be—a professional assisting in the healing process in every way. His oath is still taken by graduating medical students today.

Hippocratic medicine was practiced in the Egyptian medical school founded by two Greeks, Herophilus and Erasistratus. They dissected human bodies and learned how the organs worked. The Greeks also influenced Roman medicine. The Greek physician Galen, who was born in A.D. 130, became the most famous and influential physician in Rome. His writings on anatomy and physiology were held as the standard medical authority for centuries.

The Renaissance

With the dissolution of the Roman Empire around A.D. 400, the development of modern Western medicine was stifled for several centuries. It surged forward again after the eighth century, when the Arabs spread their empire from the Middle East to Spain, founding new medical schools and hospitals.

By the beginning of the Renaissance several centuries later, new interest was aroused in medicine. During the fifteenth century, the

Renaissance was at its pinnacle, and medicine was studied and advanced by artists like Leonardo da Vinci, who made careful drawings of the structure of the human body. Andreas Vesalius's *Fabric of the Human Body* was published in 1543. As the first printed anatomy of the human body, this work promoted the practice of surgery throughout the world.

The Seventeenth Century—Greater Understanding

During the seventeenth century, three major contributions to medicine were made. In 1628 William Harvey, an English physician, published *On the Motions of the Heart and Blood*. In it he describes his discovery of how blood circulates in the body. It has remained one of the most famous medical texts ever written because it outlines one of the most important medical discoveries ever made. Harvey also developed the study of nutrition to improve the health of the general public.

Later in the century, an Italian histologist named Marcello Malpighi filled the gap left in Harvey's discoveries by creating the first description of the capillaries that connect arteries and veins.

The Dutch scientist Anton van Leeuwenhoek refined the microscope. He used home-ground lenses with short focal lengths to observe what could not be seen before, such as red corpuscles, spermatozoa, and bacteria.

The Eighteenth Century—the Beginning of Prevention

By the eighteenth century, much was known about the workings of the human body. This century was primarily a time of systematization and classification. Carl von Linné (or Linnaeus), the Swedish botanist and physician, established the practice of classification both in botany and in medicine. He was the originator of binomial nomenclature in science, classifying each natural object by a family name and a specific name, like *Homo sapiens* for humans.

The eighteenth century witnessed great strides in the development of preventive medicine. Sanitation improved as sewers were covered and streets were paved. In 1796 Edward Jenner developed the first vaccine against smallpox. For years, smallpox epidemics had wreaked havoc with the population, killing many. When the smallpox vaccine was given to 12,000 people in London, the yearly rate of the disease dropped from 2,018 to 622.

Other important medical advances were made by Caspar Friedrich Wolff and John Hunter. Wolff, a German, is noted for his major contribution to modern embryology. Wolff noted that the embryo was not preformed and encased in the ovary, as previously believed, but rather that organs are formed "in leaf-like layers." John Hunter, a Scottish surgeon who practiced in London, was an influential physician and teacher who helped win respect for surgery as a scientific profession.

The Nineteenth Century—the Rise of Modern Medicine

Modern medicine as we know it began during the nineteenth century. The causes of many diseases were beginning to be identified, and effective treatments were being developed. The nineteenth century also brought advances in medical research and the birth of modern surgery.

One key discovery occurred when a French physician, Jean Corvisart des Marets, found that certain parts of the body have different sounds when thumped. The sound changes if fluid is present. This important diagnostic tool is called *percussing*.

Another French physician, René-Théophile Hyacinthe Laënnec, invented the stethoscope in 1819. It is said that he found percussing the chest of one of his patients too difficult, so he rolled up a cylinder of paper and placed it against the patient's chest to listen. His publication of successive editions of *Traité de l'auscultation médiate* became the foundation of modern knowledge of diseases of the chest and their diagnosis.

In 1846, at Massachusetts General Hospital in Boston, modern surgery was born when William Morton first anesthetized a patient with ether. Unfortunately, patients continued to die on the operating table from infection until chemist Louis Pasteur's discovery that bacteria caused disease was taken seriously.

The Scottish surgeon Joseph Lister understood the importance of Pasteur's discovery. Lister first tried to kill the bacteria that entered his patients during surgery. Later, he tried to prevent bacteria from entering wounds by boiling instruments and using antiseptic solutions. Also building on Pasteur's work, a German physician named Robert Koch experimented with bacteria. He identified the germ that causes tuberculosis and developed the science of bacteriology.

As the causes of disease were becoming more familiar, research into the prevention of disease flourished. The Russian bacteriologist Elie Metchnikoff discovered that certain white blood cells attack bacteria and other particles that enter the blood. In 1890 Karl Landsteiner, a German surgeon, discovered a cure for diphtheria. Landsteiner also isolated the four main blood types and made blood transfusion possible for the first time. That same year, Emil von Behring developed vaccines against tetanus and diphtheria.

The Twentieth Century—Revolutionary Progress

The twentieth century saw a tremendous explosion in the understanding and treatment of disease. Foremost among the developments was an increasingly sophisticated knowledge of how to prevent the onset and spread of illness. The technological advances of this century moved medical practice forward by leaps and bounds as well. In the early 1900s Wilhelm Roentgen began applying the use of x-rays in medicine. This radical new discovery allowed doctors to diagnose problems that previously had been invisible to them, and it advanced surgery as a science.

Another breakthrough came with the discovery of penicillin in 1928. In England, Sir Alexander Fleming discovered by chance that staphylococcus actually dissolved when exposed to *Penicillium notatum*. Fleming extracted an active principle that he called *penicillin*, which was effective in treating infection. Penicillin was eventually mass-produced in the 1940s and since then has saved millions of lives. With the introduction of the BCG vaccine and streptomycin, tuberculosis, which had been the leading cause of death in the developed world, was largely eradicated there.

Following World War II, medical research increased exponentially. Jonas Salk's polio vaccine was part of the revolutionary developments in pharmacological medicine of the 1950s and changed the face of childhood, both at home and abroad. Other drug breakthroughs of the era, such as steroids like cortisone and immunosuppressants, made it possible for doctors to tackle illnesses of the immune system and opened up the possibilities for plastic and transplant surgeries. Open-heart surgery became common in the 1950s; another leap forward, organ transplants, began in 1967.

That year Christiaan Barnard implanted a woman's heart into a man, who then lived for 18 days. By the beginning of the twenty-first century, thousands of heart transplant surgeries were being performed every year, and patients were living five years or longer with their donor hearts.

The twentieth century was also a period of unprecedented technological advances. The development of electron microscopes, endoscopes, computerized axial tomography (CAT), lasers, and other diagnostic tools radically transformed the practice of medicine. Discoveries in genetic and molecular biology, such as Francis Crick and James Watson's cracking of the genetic code in 1953, also moved medicine in a new direction.

In 1979 the world was declared free of smallpox, and in 1994 the United States was declared a polio-free zone. By the beginning of the twenty-first century, it was hard to imagine a time before mammograms became routine and before cancer could be treated with drugs, surgery, and chemotherapy.

The Future of Medicine

The monumental strides of the twentieth century helped to increase the human life span and fundamentally altered the way people look at health and illness. Never before have we lived so well, for so long. Where people once commonly died from polio, diphtheria, and smallpox, modern medicine now allows us to survive illnesses and accidents that would have been devastating in the past.

The twenty-first century promises to be an era of even greater medical progress. For those who enter the medical profession in the future, medicine will give them more tools to help their patients, but challenging ethical issues will also be raised. Questions regarding medical euthanasia, surrogate parenting, and the equitable distribution of medical resources will influence medical practice. New strains of diseases will need to be cured, and the battle against AIDS has yet to be won.

The opportunities in medicine are endless, and the need for doctors who are committed to helping others—the rich and the poor, at home and abroad—has never been greater.

2

EDUCATION AND PREPARATION

BECOMING A DOCTOR 150 years ago was considerably less complicated than it is today. Medical school lasted less than a year, and the M.D. degree was conferred regardless of grades. Although the minimum age requirement for becoming a doctor was 21, this rule was not strictly followed. Instead of intensive laboratory and clinical preparation, students learned solely by attending lectures. The medical schools of the era were proprietary schools; that is, the lecturers who instructed the students often owned the schools.

The face of medical education changed in the mid-nineteenth century as American doctors began to travel more extensively in Europe, where they were exposed to the new laboratory methods being developed by European doctors. At the same time, the modern university was emerging, and new regulatory authority was being assumed by state and federal governments. By 1910, when Abraham Flexner published his famous report that outlined the conditions in American and Canadian medical schools, the foundations of modern medical education were being established.

With the growth of medical knowledge, research and teaching became full-time activities for some in the medical profession. By the late nineteenth century, the academic physician who taught medical students was prominent. In the twenty-first century, the division between academic and clinical medicine still exists. And the medical researcher has had an impact on medical education.

Preparing for Medical School

Admission to medical school is extremely competitive. In 2003 there were about 35,000 applicants for the 16,538 available spots at the 125 medical schools in the United States. Thus, the chances of getting into medical school—any medical school—are less than 50 percent.

Most applicants want to attend what they consider the "best" medical schools. Due to the strict accreditation requirements of the Liaison Committee on Medical Education, medical schools do not vary widely in educational quality. But many factors influence the perception of medical schools, such as class size, location, clinical facilities, and other resources. It is extremely difficult to reliably rate medical schools, although the schools listed below are generally considered among the most prestigious. For that reason, admissions at these schools are even more competitive than elsewhere.

Baylor College of Medicine
Columbia University College of Physicians and Surgeons
Cornell University Weill Medical College

Duke University School of Medicine
Emory University School of Medicine
Harvard Medical School
Johns Hopkins University School of Medicine
Northwestern University Feinberg School of Medicine
Stanford University School of Medicine
University of California, Los Angeles Geffen School
    of Medicine
University of California, San Diego School of Medicine
University of California, San Francisco School of Medicine
University of Michigan Medical School
University of Pennsylvania School of Medicine
University of Pittsburgh School of Medicine
University of Texas Southwestern Medical School
University of Washington School of Medicine
Vanderbilt University School of Medicine
Washington University School of Medicine
Yale University School of Medicine

A list of all 125 U.S. and 16 Canadian accredited medical schools can be found in Appendix A. Most applicants apply to an average of 15 schools. You will have a better chance of being accepted if you carefully research schools before you choose the ones to which you apply. Most state university medical schools give preference to state residents; some do not accept any out-of-state students. If your state does not have a state-supported medical school (Alaska, Delaware, Idaho, Maine, Montana, New Hampshire, Rhode Island, Wyoming), inquire if the state has an agreement with a medical school in a neighboring state that would give you preference. The more you know about the process of applying to medical school, the better your chances of admission.

During High School

Some people know from a very young age that medicine will be their future path. While still in high school, they take their first steps down this road.

It makes sense to find out early if you like and can handle the rigorous premedical courses necessary to get into medical school. You should take difficult science courses, such as advanced placement courses, while still in high school.

Good grades and good study habits are important elements for preparing for a future in medicine. Medical school is a long and arduous process that takes more hard work than perhaps any other professional training. Developing the habits of intense studying and good time management in high school is an asset.

Even more important is finding ways to gain early exposure to the medical field. Whether you find a paid job in a lab during the summer or a volunteer position working in a hospice, you can learn a lot by being involved in the medical field before college. When you apply to medical school, these experiences will make you a more attractive candidate to admissions committees.

Joint B.S./M.D. Programs

If you are sure while you are still in high school that you want to go to medical school and you are an outstanding student, you might consider combining your undergraduate and medical studies. More than three dozen medical schools offer B.S./M.D. programs. If you are accepted into one of these programs as an undergraduate, you are automatically accepted into medical school as long as you maintain a certain grade point average as an undergraduate. Some of the programs are six years long—students begin medical school after only two years of undergraduate school. Others take seven or eight years to complete. These programs avoid the medical school application process and let students choose undergraduate courses without the constant worry about getting into medical school. The list of universities and colleges that have combined programs is found in Appendix B.

During College

Not that long ago, you had to be a science major if you wanted to go to medical school. Undergraduates used to concentrate on typical "premed" majors like biology, chemistry, and physics.

Now medical schools look for students who have a broad liberal arts education. Admissions officers are interested in applicants who have strong intellectual and communications skills, as well as a strong foundation in the sciences. Thus a major in anthropology or history will not disqualify you from acceptance.

Naturally, medical school is science intensive, and it is important that you demonstrate that you are able to handle work in the sciences. Although course requirements vary from school to school, general requirements are one year each of biology or zoology, inorganic chemistry, organic chemistry, physics, and English. The science courses should be rigorous and include sufficient laboratory experience.

Many medical schools also require or recommend calculus or college-level math courses. A few of the more prestigious medical schools require advanced-level science courses.

The Association of American Medical Colleges' publication *Medical School Admission Requirements* lists the specific undergraduate courses required by each medical school.

Postbaccalaureate Premedical Programs

For college graduates who lack the science courses needed to be admitted to medical school, more than 50 colleges and universities offer postbaccalaureate premedical programs. These programs also serve to enhance the academic record of those who want to improve the grades they got in undergraduate science courses. There are both degree and nondegree programs. Some are offered by medical schools such as Dartmouth and Drexel; others are offered by liberal arts colleges like Bryn Mawr or universities without medical schools, such as San Jose State University. A list of these programs can be found on the Association of American Medical Colleges' website at services.aamc.org/postbac.

Grade Point Average in College

It shouldn't surprise you to learn that your college grade point average is very important to the admissions officers at medical schools. They will look at both your science grade point average and your overall grade point average. Your chances of getting into the medical school of your choice increase with your grades. In 2001 the mean grade point average of accepted applicants was 3.6 (out of 4.0). Only 2 percent of students with a GPA under 2.5 were accepted to medical school. Medical schools will allow for certain special factors if you have a less than stellar GPA, for example, if you come from an educationally disadvantaged background. Nevertheless, you should strive for the highest grades possible.

Improvement in your grades in upper-class years can also work in your favor.

Applying to Medical School

The medical school application process is fraught with hope and fear for most students. Gaining admission is a combination of good grades and scores on the Medical College Admissions Test, recommendations, extracurricular activities, your personal essay, and an interview.

Most medical schools use the American Medical College Application Service (AMCAS), a centralized online application processing service. Information about AMCAS can be found on the Web at aamc.org/students/amcas/start.htm. When filling out the AMCAS form, you designate the schools to which you would like your application to be sent. These schools will evaluate your application and send you a secondary application if they are interested in considering you. On the basis of the secondary application, the medical school admissions committee will decide whether to give you an interview. After the interview, you will be accepted, rejected, or put on the waiting list. For the dozen or so medical schools that don't use the AMCAS service, you will need to apply directly to the school.

The value of good grades was mentioned earlier in this chapter. The following is a brief explanation of the other parts of the process leading to being granted an interview.

Medical College Admissions Test

The Medical College Admissions Test (MCAT) is a multiple-choice exam plus two essays administered by the Association of American

Medical Colleges. The test measures proficiency in the basic sciences, as well as general problem-solving, critical-thinking, and communications skills. The MCAT is a very important selection factor for admission to medical school.

The test is given twice a year, in April and in August. Most medical schools suggest that potential applicants take the MCAT in the spring of the year they are applying. The MCAT consists of four timed sections, including breaks, administered over a period of more than five hours. The test is given at many sites around the country, and both paper-and-pencil test sites and computer-based test sites are available.

The four sections, the number of questions in each section, and the amount of time they take to complete are shown below:

Section	Questions	Time (in minutes)
Verbal reasoning	60	85
Physical sciences	77	100
Writing sample	2	60
Biological sciences	77	100

The four sections of the MCAT are scored separately. The two essays that measure written communication skills are assigned a letter grade of J (lowest) to T (highest). The physical sciences, biological sciences, and verbal reasoning sections are scored on a scale of 1 (lowest) to 15 (highest). The average accepted medical student has scores of 9.5 in verbal reasoning, 10 in physical sciences, and 10.1 in biological sciences.

There is a wide range of review courses and practice books available to help you prepare for the MCAT. You also can receive directly from the MCAT a student manual that contains sample questions. How much time you spend preparing for the MCAT is up to you, although some people suggest that you begin up to nine months before you take the test. It is important not only to know the material and answer the questions correctly, but to do so in as little time as possible. With enough practice you can become adept at taking the test within the limited time allowed.

Recommendations

Recommendations for medical school are usually letters written by people with whom you've had an academic or professional relationship during college. If your school has premedical advising, that office will often assist you with the process of getting your letters of recommendation. Professors and physicians with whom you have worked on scientific or medically related jobs are good people to ask for letters of recommendation. At some schools, a premedical committee will draft a letter of recommendation using the letters of recommendation from individuals you have chosen to recommend you.

When requesting a letter of recommendation, you should try to approach your potential recommender with all the material he or she will need to write your recommendation. This may include a copy of your résumé, transcript, or any personal statement that you have written for your medical school application. It's always best to approach people who know your character well and understand your reasons for wanting to attend medical school.

There is no need to obtain more letters of recommendation than the schools you are applying to require. They will just add to the paperwork for the admissions committee and will not create a more favorable impression than letters from appropriate recommenders.

If you are returning to school after a few years out of college, you will need to handle the process on your own. You will still want to ask former professors for their recommendation, as medical schools will want to know about your academic readiness and intellectual ability.

Extracurricular Activities

When trying to decide if this is the profession for you, nothing can replace good old-fashioned experience. Try to find opportunities to work in a hospital, clinic, or medical research facility. Along with giving you more familiarity with the field, your extracurricular activities will also serve as an indication to admissions committees that your interest in medicine is not merely a passing fancy.

Admissions committees are always looking for more than just good grades and MCAT scores. They want to select candidates who are also caring and humane individuals. It's important to show that you are interested in pursuing a medical career for the right reasons.

The Application Essay

Medical schools request application essays because they want to get beyond the facts and figures of your grades and MCAT and find out about you as a person. Think of your personal essay as an opportunity to let them know why you want to be a doctor. A good essay will convey the relevant information about your experiences and goals. Take care to write and rewrite your essay to avoid making any sloppy errors. Have a friend or family member proofread the essay. You don't need to be a Pulitzer prize–winning writer to create a good essay, but a clear, focused essay is absolutely necessary.

Other Joint Degree Programs

Some medical schools make it possible to study for the M.D. degree concurrently with another degree. The most common program is one combining a master's degree in public health with a medical degree. Many medical schools also offer joint programs for an M.D./Ph.D. for students who want to do medical research. A few schools have programs leading to a business or law degree along with the medical degree.

Medical School Today

The field of medicine is so demanding that it is no surprise that it attracts special individuals. Those who exhibit self-discipline and maturity, as well as a genuine desire to help others, are most likely to succeed in this profession.

Increasingly, the face of medicine more closely reflects the diversity of American society. In 2004 about half of all medical students were women, and more than 30 percent of students were minorities. Among minority groups, however, only the number of Asian-American medical students equals or surpasses their proportion in the U.S. population. African-Americans, Latinos, and Native Americans are still underrepresented in medical schools. These underrepresented minorities make up about 10 percent of U.S. medical school graduates. Asian and Pacific Islanders constitute 19 percent of the graduating population, with other minority groups making up another 3 percent.

The Curriculum

Medical school generally lasts four years. During the first two years, students receive instruction in the sciences that form the core of medicine: anatomy, biochemistry, physiology, microbiology, pathology, and pharmacology, as well as the behavioral sciences. In most medical schools, students also begin to acquire practice in patient interviewing and examination techniques. Whether or not patient contact is introduced in the first year or the second year, however, almost all medical schools introduce clinical experience early in the curriculum.

In the third year, students are given more opportunities to gain experience with patients. This takes place in hospital, clinic, and office settings in the fields of internal medicine, family medicine, pediatrics, obstetrics and gynecology, surgery, and psychiatry. During the fourth and final year of medical school, students receive instruction through a combination of required and elective courses, along with more hands-on experience working with patients. The clinical clerkships of the third and fourth years allow medical students to develop their interpersonal doctor-patient skills and diagnostic abilities.

Toward the end of medical school, you will choose an area of specialization and apply to residency programs. After graduating, medical students spend at least three years in a graduate medical education program, also known as a residency. Residency programs are discussed in the next chapter; subsequent chapters discuss the different specialties and subspecialties that make up the field of medicine.

Financing Medical Education

There are a variety of loan programs available to medical school students, with ample funds provided under favorable terms. More than 80 percent of medical students graduate with debt. The amount of debt has doubled over the past 10 years as medical school tuition has increased. The average debt of 2003 graduates from medical schools in public universities was $100,000; for those graduating from medical schools in private universities it was $135,000. Some are concerned that medical students are forced to choose a medical specialty based on its income potential because of their large debts.

Although you shouldn't be discouraged from attending medical school because of cost, you should explore all options for financial aid.

Licensing Exam

The last hurdle as you begin your residency is the U.S. Medical Licensing Examination given by the National Board of Medical Examiners (nbme.org). This exam must be passed before your state medical licensing board will issue an initial license to practice medicine. Most states also require at least one year of residency before issuing a license. The first two steps of the three-step exam are taken toward the end of medical school; the last step is usually taken during the first year of residency. Although physicians licensed to practice medicine in one state can usually get a license to practice in another, some states limit reciprocity.

3

RESIDENCY TRAINING

MANY PEOPLE ENTER medical school already interested in practicing a particular kind of medicine. They may start their medical training secure in the knowledge that they will become a pediatrician, surgeon, or other specialist. During their training, they are exposed to the various branches of medicine, and while many pursue their original plans, others find they are drawn to a new specialty. In the final year of study, medical students decide in which area of medicine they want to practice. After graduating and receiving the M.D. degree, the new physicians then enter a residency program to gain expertise in the specialty of their choice. There they acquire the hands-on, practical experience that enables them to be certified by one of the 24 specialty boards.

While in 1940 there were fewer than 600 hospitals providing residency training for 5,118 physicians, by 2004 there were 98,000 residency positions distributed among 7, 900 programs. American medical schools do not graduate enough M.D.s to fill all residency positions; consequently one-quarter of all residents are graduates of foreign medical schools.

The influx of women into the medical profession is reflected in the number of female residents. In 1988, 28 percent of all residents were women. By 2002, that number had risen to 40 percent. Women are most concentrated in internal medicine, obstetrics and gynecology, pediatrics, and family medicine.

Residents, Interns, and Fellows

Residency is a period of training in a specific medical specialty. Medical organizations such as the American Medical Association (AMA) and hospitals refer to this training as graduate medical education (GME). Medical school is referred to as undergraduate medical education.

It is easy to be confused by the various terms used to describe the period of graduate medical education. In the past, medical school graduates usually spent their first graduate year in a hospital internship. For that reason, the term *intern* was used to describe individuals in their first year of hospital training. Many people still use this term when describing first-year residents in training. However, since 1975 the *Graduate Medical Education Directory* and the Accreditation Council for Graduate Medical Education have referred to them as *residents*. The first year of graduate training after medical school is called Post Graduate Year One, or PGY-1.

Another confusing term is that of *fellowship*. Fellowship is a term used by some hospitals and in some specialties to denote trainees in subspecialty GME programs. Again, however, fellows are more commonly referred to as residents. For the purpose of this text, the word *resident* will be used to describe anyone participating in graduate medical education, whether it is specialty or subspecialty training.

The National Resident Matching Program matches medical school graduates to residency programs through the Electronic Residency Application Service. More information about "the match" can be found on the Web at services.aamc.org/eras.

Location of Residency Programs

Most residency programs are based in hospitals. Residency programs might also exist in ambulatory clinics, outpatient surgical centers, mental health clinics or agencies, public health agencies, blood banks, medical examiners' offices, or physicians' offices.

Geographically, residency programs tend to be in densely populated areas of the country. The residency program's goal is to expose the new physician to as many medical or surgical situations as possible. Rural settings have less variety than urban ones and do not give the resident, especially in certain specialties and subspecialties, as rich and diverse a clinical experience. New York has the most residency programs, and California ranks second.

Specialization

There are 26 approved medical specialties. They are governed by 24 medical specialty boards that grant certification. The following is a list of these specialties:

Allergy and Immunology	Dermatology
Anesthesiology	Diagnostic Radiology
Colon and Rectal Surgery	Emergency Medicine

Family Practice
Internal Medicine
Medical Genetics
Neurological Surgery
Neurology
Nuclear Medicine
Obstetrics and Gynecology
Ophthalmology
Orthopaedic Surgery
Otolaryngology
Pathology

Pediatrics
Physical Medicine and
    Rehabilitation
Plastic Surgery
Preventive Medicine
Psychiatry
Radiation
Surgery
Thoracic Surgery
Urology

Along with these specialties are subspecialties. A subspecialist is someone who has completed specialty training and gone on to take additional training in a more specific area of that specialty. For example, nephrology, which deals with the kidneys, is a subspecialty of internal medicine; child psychiatry is a subspecialty of psychiatry; and hand surgery is a subspecialty of general surgery. These specialties and subspecialties will be discussed in greater detail in later chapters.

The length of required additional study after medical school varies from three to seven years of residency, depending on the specialty. For example, specialties such as family medicine, pediatrics, and internal medicine generally require three years of graduate medical education beyond medical school. General surgery, on the other hand, requires five years of training; other surgical specialties may call for an even longer period of residency training. Students who want to practice certain specialties frequently first enter residency programs that will provide them with a broad clinical background. Thus, a future dermatologist, radiologist, or anesthesiologist may spend the first year working as a resident in internal medicine, entering the area of specialty in the following year.

Selecting a Specialty

Potential income is one factor in determining what specialty to choose. While the median physician's income in 2003 was $187,600, in some specialties doctors can make more than $500,000 a year. Average income ranges for each specialty are given in the following chapters. However, liability (also known as malpractice) insurance costs differ by specialty and by the state in which the physician practices, and these costs have risen dramatically in the last 10 years. Some states have instituted tort reform, capping the amount of money that a patient can collect for noneconomic damages. Insurance rates are lower in these states. Some medical specialties are less invasive and, therefore, less dangerous to patients, and thus they have low insurance rates. In pathology, for example, physicians rarely even see the patient and insurance rates are low. Dermatology and psychiatry also have fairly low rates. In some specialties, your employer pays for your insurance, such as in emergency medicine. In specialties such as surgery and obstetrics/gynecology, however, liability insurance can cost hundreds of thousands of dollars in some states and, therefore, may influence what specialty a new physician will choose or where a physician will practice medicine.

Hours Worked

The number of hours a resident works depends on his or her specialty. In recent years, there has been concern that the medical care given by residents is sometimes compromised by the fact that they are exhausted from working too many hours. In 2003 the Accreditation Council for Graduate Medical Education issued new residency work-hour regulations. Residents can work a maximum of 80 hours a week. There is a 24-hour limit on continuous duty, with up to 6 hours added for continuity of patient care. Residents must have 10 hours of rest between duty periods, and one day out of seven must be free from patient care and education obligations.

Table 3.1 is drawn from physician workforce information gathered in 2002 by FREIDA (Fellowship and Residency Electronic Interactive Data Access), which is the American Medical Association's electronic database containing information about each residency program. This table shows the average hours on duty per week of several specialties, as well as the average number of consecutive hours on duty for those specialties. These hours represent the average of those worked by all residents, not just first-year residents. In fact, first-year residents sometimes put in longer hours.

Income During Residency Training

The years of residency training are not lucrative. In 2002, residents usually earned salaries in the mid-thirties to mid-forties. Some residents supplement this income with money they earn from moon-

Table 3.1 Hours of Various Physician Specialties

Specialty	Average hours on duty per week	Average maximum consecutive hours
Dermatology	42.6	14.8
Emergency medicine	54.6	18.1
Family practice	62.5	29.4
Internal medicine	64.3	27.8
Neurology	60.0	27.0
Obstetrics/gynecology	75.0	29.0
Pathology	48.8	15.7
Pediatrics	69.3	29.8
Psychiatry	52.6	27.1
Radiology	50.4	21.5
Surgery	77.2	28.3

lighting. Of course, given the intense hours worked, you should not expect to be able to dedicate much time to extra work.

Benefits are also included in residency programs. Most residents get health insurance and liability insurance as part of their benefits package. Many residents also get meals and parking as a part of the benefits they receive. Less often, residents receive housing and child care as part of the benefits package.

Board Certification

Certification is a process of testing and evaluating physicians in a medical specialty. Every specialty has its own certifying board that regulates the practice of that area of medicine. The determination of qualification is made by one of the 24 approved medical specialty boards that grant certification. These boards are listed in Appendix C. Together, these boards form the American Board of Medical Specialties (ABMS). Taking your medical boards concludes the period of residency training. Board certification consists of a written examination. Fifteen of the specialty boards require an oral exam as well. Physicians who have passed the exams of one of the specialty boards can describe themselves as "board certified." The specialty boards require continuing education in subsequent years, as physicians must periodically renew their board certification.

New Trends in Graduate Medical Education

Just as the practice of medicine is changing rapidly, so is the training of residents. Medical practice is increasingly influenced by health maintenance organizations and managed care policies. Residents must learn not only how to recognize and treat diseases and injuries, but also how to manage a patient's treatments within insurers' preestablished guidelines.

Residents still work primarily in hospitals, but they are also spending more time with patients in outpatient settings. They also work with healthy patients more than they have in the past.

The aging of America, new regulations set by the government, and breakthroughs in understanding health and disease will continue to change the way physicians learn to treat patients in the future.

4

FAMILY PRACTICE AND GENERAL INTERNAL MEDICINE

WHEN WE THINK of a family doctor, what often comes to mind is the traditional general practitioner, or G.P. Physicians in the medical specialties of family practice or internal medicine provide primary care to patients. In this chapter we'll look at the philosophy and practice of these two specialties.

Family Practice

After World War II, medical specialties began to expand rapidly. In 1940 three out of four physicians were general practitioners. By 1949 only two out of three were G.P.s.

Medicine was changing. Medical staffs were beginning to require board certification for physicians with hospital privileges. As the specialists gained status and popularity, general practitioners were left behind.

When general practitioners began to take steps to improve their diminishing status, they knew that one of the hallmarks of their practices was the interaction with patients and their families. So, the terms *family physician* and *family practice* began to emerge. By 1969, family practice was a board certified specialty. The next year, more than 12,000 physicians were designated as specialists in family practice. By 2004, that number had risen to more than 66,000, of whom 32 percent were women.

The Profession

The American Board of Family Practice (ABFP) defines family practice this way:

> Family practice is the medical specialty which is concerned with the total health care of the individual and the family. It is the specialty in breadth which integrates the biological, clinical, and behavioral sciences. The scope of family practice is not limited by age, sex, organ system, or disease entity.

The family practitioner cares for people from the time they are still in the womb (more than 20 percent deliver babies) through old age. The family physician is trained to provide comprehensive medical and surgical care, also called primary care, to entire families. If a problem is beyond the scope of a family physician, he or she will refer the patient to another physician who specializes in the particular problem.

Even if a family physician does not treat a whole family, he or she always approaches medicine within the context of a family. In other words, a family practitioner always considers the patient as a social person, living within a family grouping of one sort or another. That means putting emphasis on the disease patterns found within the family and paying attention to an individual's lifestyle.

Medical students are often attracted to family practice because of the diversity of the field. They can diagnose and treat and oversee a patient's continuing progress.

Close and continuing relationships are also an attractive part of the family practice specialty. Most family physicians enjoy forming personal connections with their patients, whom they may know for decades. Family physicians thus are in a unique position to treat the "whole person," as they deal with their physical, emotional, and social health.

Every specialty has its drawbacks, and family practice is no exception. Because of the nature of the care they provide, family physicians put in long hours. Because of their close relationships with patients, family practitioners are called on outside of regular business hours and sometimes have interrupted personal lives as a result.

Their wide range of skills also brings family physicians into direct competition for patients with other physicians. The specialties they most often overlap with are internal medicine, obstetrics and gynecology, and pediatrics.

Despite the long hours and hard work, family physicians make less money than other physicians do. The average annual gross income for all physicians is approximately $187,600. The average gross income of a family physician ranges from $146,000 to $165,000. Liability insurance premiums for family physicians tend to be lower than those for most medical specialties.

Training

In 1970 there were only 49 approved residency programs in family practice; by 2002 there were 481. The American Board of Family Practice requires successful completion of a three-year residency program. The only prerequisite for entry to a residency program in family practice is the completion of the M.D. degree.

Residents diagnose and treat both inpatients (patients who are staying in the hospital) and outpatients (patients who are not hospitalized). As they progress through their training, residents take increasing responsibility for all aspects of patient care.

In addition, family practice training emphasizes preventive medicine, community medicine, and application of the understanding of human behavior to the day-to-day practice of medicine. Family practice was the first specialty board requiring periodic recertification, using a written test at six-year intervals.

As the population of the United States lives longer, there is a greater need for family practice–based geriatric programs. This led in 1985 to the creation of an additional certificate program for physicians with an interest in geriatrics. Fellowship programs based in family practice residencies are also available in obstetrics, sports medicine, and other clinical and educational areas.

In 2002 there were 9,603 residents in training in family practice. Almost 50 percent were women.

Internal Medicine

The term *internal medicine* was used by German physicians late in the nineteenth century to describe a branch of medicine that did not use surgical methods of treatment with patients.

The American Congress on Internal Medicine was established in 1915 to facilitate exchange of ideas among physicians interested in this branch of medicine, to publish, and to grant research fellowships. This group became today's professional association, the American College of Physicians. In 2003 there were more than 164,000 internists in the United States.

The Profession

Specialists in internal medicine primarily treat adults, although some also treat adolescents. Internists, as they are often called, intimately understand all the major organ systems. They diagnose and treat acute and chronic diseases, usually from practices based in offices. They also visit patients hospitalized for problems that fall under the domain of internal medicine.

Every day internists see and treat a wide range of patients with a great array of illnesses. A typical day might see an internist treating colds and flu as well as diabetes and heart problems.

In medical school it is often said that internal medicine is an intellectual medical specialty because internists often diagnose and treat based on discussion with their patients, rather than relying on extensive tests and procedures.

Some internists are board certified in internal medicine and another internal medicine specialty, such as cardiology or gastroenterology. This enables these physicians to have a general internal medicine practice, but also to be experts in a particular aspect of internal medicine.

Like family practice, internal medicine offers close and long-term relationships with patients. An internist is often in charge of overall patient management because of this relationship. If a patient has a problem that requires specialty treatment, the internist often coordinates that care. Internal medicine can be a challenging specialty because of the diversity and intellectual stimulation it offers to its practitioners.

Like family practitioners, internists must make themselves available to their patients, sometimes outside of business hours. They may sacrifice more of their personal lives than physicians in other specialties.

Despite the long hours and degree of responsibility, internists are not among the highest paid physicians. Their average annual gross income ranges from $150,000 to $179,000. However, their liability premiums tend to be lower than those of many other physicians. In 2002, internists paid an average of $12,355 for insurance, just a little higher than what family practitioners pay. In 2003, premiums ranged from $2,786 in Nebraska to $65,700 in Florida.

Training

Residency training for general internal medicine takes three years. The prerequisite to training is the completion of the M.D. degree. In 2002 there were 21,136 residents being trained at 392 accredited residency programs in internal medicine. Of these, 40 percent were women. Board certification is granted through the American Board of Internal Medicine.

There has been a decrease over the last decade in the number of internal medicine residency positions filled by U.S. medical school graduates. The factors for this decrease are numerous. They include an increase in the number of foreign-trained doctors who now sometimes fill residency positions in internal medicine.

Also, the rates at which insurance companies and the government reimburse primary care physicians for medical treatment are not as high as they are in some other subspecialties. Interviewing patients and making a diagnosis, both of which are a large part of a primary care practice, are often not reimbursed at as high a rate as procedures that are more technological in nature. Therefore, this reimbursement system may be creating a financial disincentive for students to become primary care physicians.

There are many subspecialties and certificates that are encompassed by internal medicine. The following chapter is an introduction to these subspecialties.

5

INTERNAL MEDICINE SUBSPECIALTIES

INTERNAL MEDICINE ENCOMPASSES a number of subspecialties. These subspecialties involve different organ systems, particular age groups, or other areas of expertise. As medicine has progressed, new subspecialties have been added to the list. You can expect that by the time you are ready to choose a specialty or subspecialty, the range of options will have again expanded, reflecting the dynamic nature of the medical profession. In the last 10 years, for example, it has become possible for physicians to be certified in the specialties of nuclear medicine and medical genetics.

Cardiovascular Medicine

Cardiovascular diseases are the leading cause of death in the United States. Therefore, the subspecialist in cardiovascular medicine—the cardiologist or heart specialist—is in great demand for his or her expertise.

Cardiology is the subspecialty dedicated to diagnosing and treating diseases and malfunctions of the heart, lungs, and blood vessels. It is a highly challenging and intellectual discipline of medicine, combining diagnostic detective work with a thorough mastery of highly technological procedures.

As heart specialists, cardiologists treat largely middle-aged and elderly people. Pediatric cardiology, which treats children with congenital heart defects, is a subspecialty of pediatrics. Because of the significance of the heart in the human body, cardiologists are often right in the thick of things both when patients have chronic illnesses and when they experience life-and-death emergencies.

Although in past years cardiology was primarily a diagnostic and medically oriented specialty, advances in the field have facilitated more invasive procedures. An example of this trend is cardiac catheterization, whereby a patient, under local anesthetic in an operating room, has dye injected into the arteries so that the cardiologist may locate any blockages. This type of complicated invasive procedure has brought some cardiologists closer to being surgeons than they were before. As a result, cardiologists now divide themselves into two groups, invasive and noninvasive, depending upon how they practice the subspecialty. Common conditions that cardiologists treat include coronary artery disease, heart attacks, hypertension, life-threatening abnormal heart rhythms, and stroke.

In addition to diagnosis and high-tech intervention, cardiologists also place a high premium on prevention and are at the forefront of the preventive medicine frontier. Advances in knowledge about nutrition and exercise have helped reduce the number of deaths from heart disease.

Medical students who are interested in cardiology are often attracted by the challenge of this quickly evolving field. It is a subspecialty where diagnosis, high-tech progress, and prevention all meet. Cardiologists have a combination of long-term relationships with some patients and consultative roles with others.

Cardiology can be a stressful area of medicine. Sometimes cardiologists deal with very sick people who cannot be helped. Because of the life-and-death aspects of their subspecialty, cardiologists often deal with problems that can't wait, and these can interrupt the cardiologist's personal life.

There were 1,999 residents training in 175 accredited programs in cardiology in 2002. Of these, 17 percent were women. Training in cardiology includes three years of a general internal medicine residency with three additional years of training in cardiology.

Although there has been steady growth in the number of cardiologists, a larger elderly population is likely to increase the demand for their services in the future. Most cardiologists have private practices from which they treat patients. In the past, most cardiologists' practices were solo practices. There has been a shift recently toward group practices. About one-third of a cardiologist's time with patients is spent on hospital rounds. Many of their hospitalized patients are in special units called coronary care or cardiac units. A small percentage of cardiologists are researchers only; there are many opportunities for cardiologists in research. The average salary for a cardiologist is far higher than that of many other specialties.

Endocrinology and Metabolism

Endocrinologists diagnose and treat illnesses and disorders of the hormone-producing glandular and metabolic systems. Endocrinologists see a wide variety of diseases and have patients who range from the very sick to those who need minimal treatment. Endocrinologists are also often researchers, blending clinical medicine with research. Endocrinology is unique, as few other specialties involve the same level of active research on the part of practitioners.

Endocrinology requires broad knowledge of other fields of medicine. Endocrinologists treat such disorders as thyroid conditions, diabetes, pituitary disorders, calcium disorders, sexual problems, nutritional disorders, and hypertension. Because of the nature of some of the diseases they treat, such as diabetes, there is an educational component in their treatment, as endocrinologists teach patients with an ongoing condition how to manage their illnesses.

Endocrinologists work long hours. However, the analytical nature of the subspecialty is what attracts medical students and residents. Rapidly developing technology in endocrinology also challenges those pursuing it.

In 2002 there were 437 residents training at 118 accredited programs in endocrinology. Female residents made up 51 percent of this total. Three years of internal medicine residency are required with an additional two years in endocrinology and metabolism.

Gastroenterology

Gastroenterologists diagnose and treat disorders of, or relating to, the digestive system. This includes the stomach, bowels, liver, gallbladder, and related organs. Gastroenterologists treat such diseases as cirrhosis of the liver, hepatitis, ulcers, cancer, jaundice, inflammatory bowel disease, and irritable bowel disease. Their caseloads are mostly made up of adults and the elderly, with infants and children forming only a very small percentage of their patient populations.

Gastroenterology is a procedures-oriented specialty. It requires a high degree of motor skill and manual dexterity. It involves medical investigation, and gastroenterologists enjoy a good mix of patient care, diagnostic challenges, and procedures.

Some gastroenterologists say that a frustrating part of their field is dealing with patients who do not comply with treatments or with patients who wait so long for treatment that nothing can be done. It is also troubling to some that the procedures they must do are physically uncomfortable for their patients. These procedures include endoscopy, where the physician examines the intestines through lighted endoscopes. With an endoscope the gastroenterologist can biopsy tissue and remove small growths.

Because of invasive procedures like endoscopy, gastroenterology is more surgical than it used to be. Gastroenterologists' level of responsibility is very high because of the invasiveness of some of the procedures they perform.

Gastroenterology is a lucrative field, although the hours are long and there are emergency consultations on nights and weekends.

In 2002 there were 1,058 residents in 155 accredited training programs in gastroenterology. Of these, 22 percent were women. Gastroenterologists must finish three years of training in internal medicine and complete another two years in gastroenterology.

Hematology

Hematology is the subspecialty that deals with blood, blood diseases, and the spleen and lymph glands. Hematologists are researchers as well as clinicians. Many hematology training programs are connected to medical oncology programs, which treat cancer.

Hematologists treat all organ systems, but always related to the blood in those systems. They treat all age groups. This is a rapidly advancing field, and diagnosis and treatment often involve the use of high-tech equipment.

Blood diseases are often serious or fatal, and physicians pursuing this field must be prepared for the stresses of dealing with critically ill patients. Hematologists must contend with the ongoing strain of death, even in the young, but not lose their compassion in the process. The rewarding aspect of this specialty comes with improving patients' lives. Hematologists treat leukemia, other cancers of the blood, lymphoma, sickle-cell disease, hemophilia, serious anemia, and secondary problems that arise when a patient has another type of cancer. They also perform blood transfusions and biopsies on bone marrow.

Like many other subspecialties of internal medicine, hematology is analytical and highly intellectual. Because of the research and writing involved in hematology, it is a valuable asset if the person choosing this field is a good writer. This subspecialty is a demanding one, so personal time can be limited.

There were 74 residents working in 20 accredited training programs in hematology in 2002. Women made up 61 percent of hematology residents. Hematologists must finish three years of training in general internal medicine and complete another two years in a hematology training program.

Infectious Disease

Subspecialists in infectious disease diagnose and treat communicable disease. Traditionally, most infectious disease subspecialists worked in hospitals or medical centers, where difficult cases are referred. Today, however, there are more opportunities for private practice in this field. Infectious disease specialists are usually found in urban areas, where they can receive referrals from a large number of other physicians.

This is an intellectually challenging field that requires detective work. People are usually referred to these specialists when other physicians can't determine the cause of the problem. For instance, when a person has a fever that cannot be explained, the patient is often referred to an infectious disease specialist. The field of infectious disease is very diverse, requiring the practitioner to have a wide range of clinical expertise. This specialty has changed dramatically in recent years with the advent of AIDS.

An infectious disease practice does not involve a lot of procedures. For that reason, infectious disease specialists are not as well-paid as some of the more procedures-oriented specialists. As infectious diseases are transmitted from person to person, usually through some form of contact, there is also a public health aspect to this subspecialty when outbreaks occur and affect whole populations of people. Most infectious disease specialists do not form long-lasting relationships with patients, with the notable exception of the case of AIDS, whereby the infectious disease specialist sometimes becomes the primary care physician.

There were 625 residents in training at 139 accredited training programs in infectious disease in 2002, 43 percent of whom were women. Three years of internal medicine residency are mandatory, followed by at least two years of subspecialty training in infectious diseases.

Medical Oncology

Medical oncology deals with tumors and cancers, which can occur in all organ systems. This subspecialty is closely related to hematology. It is a multidisciplinary field because the medical oncologist treats all or any systems, and oncologists often consult with specialists in those systems. Oncology is a rapidly expanding and ever-changing discipline, and research opportunities in oncology are plentiful.

Oncologists who primarily treat patients must face the problems associated with close contact with seriously or terminally ill patients. There is a high patient mortality rate, and persons entering this field must find ways to handle the stress of dealing with death more than most other physicians. It is important in oncology to have a support system of one's own to help with the emotional aspects.

However, oncology also provides lots of opportunities for getting to know patients well and having a high degree of involvement in their lives. Medical oncologists are often very involved with patients' families, too.

Because no two cases are alike, and because all organ systems are involved, the field of oncology is very diverse. Oncologists work on specific, practical problems and also examine larger, more theoretical issues. They are required to know a great deal about all aspects of medicine, and must depend upon referrals from other physicians.

There were 199 residents in 121 training programs in oncology in 2002. Women made up 33 percent of oncology residents. After a three-year residency in general internal medicine, an additional two years of subspecialty training in oncology are required.

Nephrology

Nephrology is the treatment of diseases and malfunctions of the kidneys and the urinary system. Nephrologists provide care for patients with kidney disorders, fluid and mineral imbalances, renal failure, and diabetes. They are involved with dialysis and consultation with surgeons about kidney transplantation.

Nephrologists see chronically ill patients, and they must have a broad-based knowledge of general internal medicine. However, like some other subspecialists in general internal medicine, they must also face the challenges of treating some very sick patients. Many nephrologists have patients who wait for many years for a kidney to become available for transplantation, for example.

Nephrologists, because they treat chronic diseases, get to know patients and their families well. There is a high level of continuous care in this field.

Like many other subspecialties of internal medicine, nephrology is as diverse as it is intellectually challenging. Many facets of science and medicine are applied in nephrology: the basic sciences, chemistry, physics, and good people skills.

There were 711 residents in 128 accredited training programs in nephrology in 2002. Of these, 31 percent were women. Along with a three-year residency in general internal medicine, an additional two-year residency in nephrology is required.

Pulmonary Medicine

Pulmonary medicine is the treatment of disorders of the respiratory system. Pulmonary specialists, called pulmonologists, treat the lungs and other chest tissues. Pulmonologists treat cancer, pneumonia, occupational diseases, bronchitis, emphysema, asthma, and other lung disorders. They may test lung functions, probe into the bronchial airways, and manage mechanical breathing assistance. Pulmonologists often are found in critical care units of hospitals.

There is a lot of variety in pulmonary medicine, and pulmonologists consult with patients, perform procedures, and practice high-tech interventions. They see patients in outpatient practices as well as in the hospital. Like many of the subspecialties in internal medicine, the hours are very long. Because of the nature of their specialty, pulmonologists spend a lot of time in consultation with other physicians.

In 2002 there were 114 residents in 100 accredited programs in pulmonary medicine. Women made up 24 percent of pulmonary residents. After a three-year residency in general internal medicine, an additional two years of training in pulmonary medicine are required.

Rheumatology

Rheumatologists diagnose and treat joint, muscle, and skeletal problems, including arthritis, muscle strains, athletic injuries, and back pain. They also deal with autoimmune diseases, such as lupus, which may have rheumatologic symptoms.

This is a rapidly evolving field. Rheumatologists are involved in prevention because some of the diseases they treat have been linked to lifestyle or nutritional problems. Because of the chronic nature of many of the diseases they treat, rheumatologists tend to have long-term, close relationships with their patients. Many rheumatologists say it is important to have good listening ability and compassion, as many of the diseases they treat, such as rheumatoid arthritis, are very painful. Rheumatologists are, to a higher degree than some other subspecialties in internal medicine, involved in the management of pain.

Rheumatologists can have more regular hours than many of their colleagues because there is little critical care involved. Many rheumatologists have office-based practices.

In 2002 there were 307 active residents in 106 accredited programs in rheumatology. Women made up 52 percent of rheumatology residents. Three years of residency in general internal medicine are required, along with an additional two years of training in rheumatology.

Other Subspecialties

Other areas of internal medicine include newer subspecialties. Three of these new subspecialties are critical care medicine, geriatric medicine, and clinical and laboratory immunology.

Critical Care Medicine

Critical care medicine involves management of life-threatening, acute disorders—mostly in intensive care units. Critical care specialists take care of patients with shock, coma, heart failure, respiratory arrest, drug overdose, massive bleeding, diabetic acidosis, and kidney shutdown. Critical care is a subspecialty of these specialty boards: internal medicine, anesthesiology, neurological surgery, obstetrics and gynecology, and general surgery.

Geriatric Medicine

Although most subspecialties treat the elderly, geriatric medicine offers physicians the opportunity to intimately understand the needs of the elderly. As the baby boom generation ages, the percentage of Americans 65 and older will double, reaching 70 million by the year 2030. Only about 8,000 geriatricians were in practice at the end of the twentieth century, but it is predicted that the country will need as many as 36,000 in coming years.

The subspecialty of geriatric medicine is sponsored jointly by family practice and internal medicine. Practitioners must be familiar with the particular needs and treatments of an elderly client base, as well as understanding how to use resources such as nursing homes and social services to care for the elderly.

Clinical and Laboratory Immunology

Clinical and laboratory immunology is a subspecialty of allergy and immunology, pediatrics, and internal medicine. These subspecialists perform laboratory tests and complex procedures that are used to diagnose and treat diseases and conditions resulting from defective immune systems.

6

SURGERY AND SURGICAL SPECIALTIES

THE MODERN SURGEON uses an astonishing array of sophisticated techniques and tools, but this was not always the case. At one time, barber surgeons used their razors to open veins for bloodletting. The term "surgeon" was originally *chirurgeon*, from the Greek word *cheir*, meaning hand, and *ergon*, meaning work. In the eighteenth century in Europe, surgeons were seen as socially inferior to other physicians. In fact, very few surgeons had university degrees. While physicians were addressed as "doctor," surgeons were addressed as "mister," and this is still the case in Great Britain today.

Surgery has come a long way from the early days. Today, general surgeons and those in eight other surgical specialties are highly trained, well-respected, well-paid members of the medical community. In this chapter, we will discuss these nine specialties.

General Surgery

General surgery involves all types of surgical operations. Although general surgeons have heavy competition from the other surgical specialties, general surgery remains one of the most popular areas of specialization. It is often said in medical school that those who go into surgery seek clear-cut answers and results. They don't like the ambiguities and gray areas that arise in internal medicine and enjoy the direct intervention of surgery.

A surgeon's hours can be long, irregular, and grueling. When a patient needs surgery, the surgeon must be there, day or night. Surgery is not a specialty that creates many long-term relationships between doctor and patient. Ideally, patients who need an operation improve after surgery and no longer need the surgeon's expertise. Follow-up care will often be given by the patient's primary care physician. Conditions that a surgeon typically treats include gallbladder disease, hernia, appendicitis, breast cancer, and cancers of the digestive system.

The surgeon handles everything from minor health problems to profoundly serious diseases. Surgeons operate on patients of all ages, but because of the subspecialty of pediatric surgery, in some areas of the country they treat mostly adults. There is a considerable amount of pressure in all surgical subspecialties because of the nature of the work and the responsibility that is placed upon surgeons.

The average gross annual income of general surgeons in 2003 ranged from $217,000 to $291,000 a year. Surgeons make excellent incomes, but many have high expenses. Average annual liability premiums for surgeons are $36,564, for example. In 2003, premiums ranged from a high of $226,500 in Florida to a low of $8,717 in Minnesota.

In 2002 there were 7,412 residents working in 253 accredited residency programs in general surgery. Women made up 24 percent of this total. A five-year residency in general surgery is required by the American Board of Surgery. Residents can begin their surgery training immediately upon graduating from medical school, without doing a residency in internal medicine first.

Colon and Rectal Surgery

Colon and rectal surgeons deal with diseases of the intestinal tract, anus, and rectum. Until 1961 this specialty was called proctology because of the root *proctos*, the Greek word for anus. The name was changed to reflect the broader scope of the specialty.

Colon and rectal surgeons treat all age groups but primarily work with middle-aged and older patients. Although they are surgeons, these specialists perform a mix of medical and surgical procedures. An average day may involve some surgery but also diagnostic techniques such as endoscopy, discussed in Chapter 5 under the section on gastroenterology. Colon and rectal surgeons treat hemorrhoids, fissures, polyps, cancer, colitis, and diverticulitis. Many of these diseases and conditions are easy to diagnose, and treatment has a high rate of success.

One of the most positive aspects of becoming a colon and rectal surgeon is the lack of emergency situations, so these surgeons have more control of their hours than do surgeons in many other specialties. Hours in this specialty are fairly regular. There is a good diversity of patients, ranging from the uncomfortable to the very sick. Colon and rectal surgeons can give quick relief to patients who are suffering from painful conditions.

Physicians in this specialty work out of their offices as well as in the hospital. A high degree of manual dexterity is required for this specialty, both because surgery is so exacting and for the diagnostic procedures used.

There are also opportunities for research in this field. New techniques for care and preventive measures for colon and rectal cancer are constantly being sought. Although their area of expertise is narrowly focused, the prerequisite training in general surgery gives these specialists a good working knowledge of internal medicine. This is important because many conditions that colon and rectal specialists treat originate elsewhere in the body.

Average salaries range from $158,000 to $318,000 a year for practitioners. The field of gastroenterology is related to this field.

Colon and rectal surgeons have one of the longest training programs in medicine. Completion of a five-year program in general surgery is a prerequisite to a one- or two-year residency in colon and rectal surgery. There were only 60 residents active at 37 accredited training programs in 2002; 14 percent were women.

Neurological Surgery

Neurological surgery, better known as neurosurgery, is the diagnosis, evaluation, and treatment of disorders of the central, peripheral, and autonomic nervous systems. Practitioners use high-tech equipment such as magnetic resonance imaging (MRI) to diagnose problems. They also meet with patients for regular physical examination in the office.

This can be a highly stressful and demanding specialty because it deals with the brain. The variation in outcomes is great; there are remarkable interventions and profound disappointments, as when a patient dies despite heroic intervention. The brain is a fascinating organ, and we are just beginning to understand its mysteries.

The threat of malpractice is greater in neurosurgery than in some other specialties; as a result, insurance premiums are extremely high, as much as $300,000 a year in some states. The hours are long, and because neurosurgeons treat accidents and brain disorders that erupt suddenly, they may be called at any hour of the day. Yet neurosurgery is challenging, creative, and constantly changing. Because of the serious nature of the problems neurosurgeons deal with, practitioners get to know their patients well.

A good deal of manual dexterity and technical skill is required. Neurosurgeons treat brain and spinal cord cancers, hydrocephalus, lumbar and cervical disc disease, aneurysms, and head and spinal cord trauma. Neurosurgeons must be excellent problem solvers, and they must also understand the logic of anatomy, physiology, and integration of the nervous system.

Neurosurgeons see a wide variety of conditions and serve a range of ages. They move between hospital visits, the operating room, and office settings.

Neurosurgeons rank among the highest paid specialists, often earning more than $400,000 a year. However, expenses, such as liability premiums, can be very high.

In 2002 there were 778 residents at 94 accredited training programs in neurosurgery. Of these residents, 11 percent were women. A year of a general surgery residency is required as well as a five-year residency in neurosurgery.

Ophthalmology

Ophthalmology is one of several surgical specialties without the word *surgery* in its title. Ophthalmology brings surgical, medical, and diagnostic prowess to the diseases and abnormalities of the eye.

Ophthalmologists deal with sight loss, conjunctivitis, glaucoma, macular degeneration, and cataracts. They treat the very young to the very old. Because they work on such a small and delicate part of the body—the eye—ophthalmologists must possess excellent eye-hand coordination and technical skill. Ophthalmologists must be knowledgeable about optics, refraction, and visual physiology.

While some of their patients are seen for only one procedure, ophthalmologists often have long-term relationships with patients who have vision problems. Because they face few life-and-death situations, ophthalmologists deal very little with ethical issues like the right to die.

Ophthalmologists spend time in office treatment as well as in the operating room. They have some overlap with optometrists, who are not M.D.s and who have their own schools of optometry not related to medical school.

Ophthalmologists' hours are much more controlled than are those in many other specialties. Annual average gross income ranges from $129,000 to $287,000, and liability insurance premiums are about average.

There were 1,290 residents in 121 accredited training programs in ophthalmology in 2002. Of these, 34 percent were women. Ophthalmologists must have one year of general residency training, followed by at least three years of an ophthalmology residency.

Orthopaedic Surgery

According to the American Board of Orthopaedic Surgeons:

> Orthopaedic surgery is the medical specialty that includes the preservation, investigation, and restoration of the form and function of the extremities, spine, and associated structures by medical, surgical, and physical methods.

Orthopaedic surgeons, sometimes referred to as orthopods, often have broad-based practices, but they may choose a narrower focus such as hand surgery or sports medicine. It is often said that orthopaedic surgeons are mechanically inclined and like to put things together. The manual dexterity that they need serves not only in microsurgery, delicate spine surgery, and hip replacements, but also serves the practitioner well during casting and manipulation of fractures. Physical strength is necessary for some procedures.

Conditions that orthopaedic surgeons commonly treat include arthritis, fractures, knee trauma, lower back pain, hip trauma, shoulder injuries, deformities, and degenerative diseases of the hip, knees, hands, feet, shoulders, and elbows. Because this specialty often deals with accident victims, there is a certain amount of time spent in assessing disability in legal actions.

One of the most positive aspects about being an orthopaedic surgeon is the ability to quickly relieve pain and to see patients leave satisfied and in good condition. There are lots of positive outcomes in orthopaedic surgery. Orthopaedic surgeons see a wide range of problems and a wide range of patients. It is as common to see children as it is to see the elderly.

Orthopaedic surgeons can work very long hours, sometimes 12 to 15 hours a day. This detracts from a personal life. Their income level, however, is high. Average gross income ranges from $190,000 to $364,000. But liability premiums are quite high, and the cost of office equipment, such as x-ray machines, is part of the overhead necessary.

In 2002 there were 3,002 residents in 152 accredited orthopaedic training programs. Women made up 9 percent of orthopaedic residents. Up to two years are required in a general surgery or other approved medical or surgical residency. Three years are required after that in an orthopaedic residency.

Otolaryngology

This surgical specialty used to be called ENT—ear, nose, and throat, or otorhinolaryngology. In 1980 the name of the specialty was changed to otolaryngology—head and neck surgery. This specialty deals with surgery of everything above the shoulders. The exceptions are eye disorders, which are treated by ophthalmologists, and brain disorders, which are treated by neurologists and neurosurgeons.

Otolaryngologists see patients of all ages. Their specialty requires a range of skills because they treat a variety of problems both medically and surgically. Common conditions that otolaryngologists treat include hearing loss, tonsillitis, sinusitis, and head and neck cancers. Their surgical procedures are widely varied because they perform plastic surgery, delicate microsurgery, laser surgery, and major reconstructive procedures.

Otolaryngologists can be in competition with other specialties for patients. The specialties of thoracic surgery, plastic surgery, allergy and immunology, and pulmonary medicine particularly overlap with theirs. Some otolaryngologists solve this by becoming super-specialists, specializing only in facial plastic surgery, for instance, or otology (relating to disorders of the ear).

Otolaryngologists typically have fairly normal working hours and fewer emergencies than many other specialties experience. Annual average gross income ranges from $155,000 to $304,000.

In 2002 there were 1,093 residents in 102 accredited training programs in otolaryngology, of whom 20 percent were female. One or two years of general surgery are required before entering an otolaryngology training program, which takes three or four years to complete.

Plastic Surgery

While plastic surgeons are perhaps best known for their cosmetic work on aging movie stars, much of their work takes place outside the domain of vanity. Plastic surgeons help those born with deformities or burn victims regain a normal appearance. In addition to rhinoplasty for the nose and liposuction for the thighs, plastic surgeons treat a variety of clinical disorders such as cancer, congenital deformities, skin lesions, facial trauma, and degenerative diseases.

This is a highly creative field that requires a good aesthetic sense, attention to detail, and the ability to visualize and imagine. It is also a very innovative field with many new procedures on the horizon like artificial skin for burn patients and fat transfers.

Since plastic surgeons often improve people's appearance, they can gain a great deal of satisfaction from having happy patients; but one pitfall in this field can be patients' unrealistic expectations. Plastic surgeons see a wide variety of problems and a range of ages. While they sometimes have ongoing relationships with patients, most often they perform one or a few procedures on a patient and the relationship is over.

A high degree of manual dexterity is needed to be a plastic surgeon. The intellectual demands of the field usually come before the procedure; the plastic surgeon calculates the strategy ahead of time. Plastic surgeons require a combination of resourcefulness, artistic talent, and people skills.

Plastic surgery is very competitive. There are other specialists who perform some of the same procedures, like dermatologists who do skin grafts or otolaryngologists who do face-lifts. There is a great variance in number of hours worked; plastic surgeons who are on-call in a busy emergency room may have long hours, while those who have private practices have more controllable schedules. Average annual gross income for plastic surgeons ranges from $153,000 to $410,000.

In 2002 there were 531 residents in 88 accredited plastic surgery training programs, and 26 percent of them were women. The route to becoming a plastic surgeon offers options. Prerequisites are a three-to-five-year residency in general surgery, otolaryngology, or orthopaedics. A plastic surgery residency, after the prerequisite is satisfied, lasts at least two years. Many programs require physicians to do a five- or six-year residency in plastic surgery if they have not completed residencies in any of the various prerequisite specialties.

Thoracic Surgery

Thoracic surgery deals with surgery of the chest cavity, heart, lungs, and esophagus. It is a highly specialized and demanding field and requires decisiveness and the ability to make life-and-death decisions. This specialty demands great manual dexterity and stamina. The hours are long, and the threat of malpractice is greater than in many other specialties.

Common conditions that thoracic surgeons treat are lung cancer, coronary artery disease, aneurysms, and heart disease. While patients of thoracic surgeons can be very ill, surgery can often result in immediate and sometimes dramatic improvement. Thoracic surgeons have a combination of long-term and short-term relationships with patients.

Thoracic surgeons' level of income is high. Average annual gross income ranges from $196,000 to $496,000. However, liability premiums are also very high.

In 2002 there were 316 residents in 91 accredited training programs in thoracic surgery. Women made up only 8 percent of thoracic surgery residents. It requires the longest residency of any specialty. A five-year general surgery residency is followed by two or three years of a thoracic surgery residency.

Urology

Although urology does not have the word *surgery* attached to it, it is a surgical specialty. Urology deals with the medical and surgical treatment of disorders of the female urinary tract and the male urogenital tract. Urology relies heavily on diagnostic procedures, and medical intervention can be as significant in treatment as surgery. Common conditions that urologists treat include prostate conditions, malignancies in the genitourinary tract, urinary tract infections, and bladder disorders.

Urologists work with a range of disorders from the very serious to the merely uncomfortable. Many available interventions can dramatically improve a patient's condition. There are many newer treatments in urology including short, easier treatments for urinary incontinence, prostatic ultrasound, shock wave lithotripsy, and endoscopic surgery. Urologists need coordination and manual dexterity to perform their responsibilities.

Urologists work primarily with adults and the elderly. They often have long-term relationships with patients. Because they combine medical and surgical treatment, they divide their time between the office and the hospital. Urologists have long hours, but their income is very comfortable. Average annual gross salary ranges from $243,000 to $334,000.

In 2002 there were 1,009 residents in 120 accredited training programs in urology. Of these, 13 percent were women. A minimum of five years of residency is required. The first two years are usually in general surgery.

7

OTHER SPECIALTIES

THE PREVIOUS CHAPTERS discussed general medical and surgical specialties. There are fourteen additional specialties and many more subspecialties. Two of these specialties, pediatrics and obstetrics/gynecology, are primary care specialties. In primary care, patients and their physicians often form ongoing relationships. There are other specialties, however, that many people never have occasion to use.

Anesthesiology is an older specialty. Although most people know that anesthesiologists are the doctors who put you to sleep before surgery, very few people understand the other tasks performed by anesthesiologists. Nuclear medicine is a newer specialty that employs the exploding technology of the past few decades. An even newer specialty is medical genetics, which probes the genetic causes of illnesses and seeks cures in genetic therapies. The other specialties covered in this chapter are allergy and immunology, dermatology, emergency medicine, neurology, pathology, physical medicine and rehabilitation, preventive medicine, psychiatry, and radiology.

Pediatrics

Pediatricians care for infants, children, and teens. Pediatricians see mostly healthy children, providing well-child care and guidance on prevention of illness.

Pediatrics is a specialty that calls for strong interpersonal skills, as pediatricians must deal with children and their parents. It is a demanding branch of medicine that includes long hours and interruptions in the evenings.

Pediatric patients respond well to treatment and are often happy and satisfied customers. Children heal faster than adults, and this aspect of pediatrics can be very gratifying.

Although most of their work is with healthy children, pediatricians do see a variety of disorders. These include throat and respiratory infections, communicable diseases, cancer, congenital abnormalities, and developmental and behavioral problems. Pediatricians practice mostly in offices, sometimes in private practice and sometimes in alternative settings like health maintenance organizations (HMOs). They also make hospital visits when they have very ill patients.

Like many of the specialties that are contact-intensive rather than procedures-intensive, pediatricians make less money than many of their colleagues. Average annual gross salary ranges from $145,000 to $168,000. Malpractice premiums are fairly low.

In 2002 there were 7,699 residents in 207 accredited programs in pediatrics. Women accounted for 65 percent of all pediatric residents in 2002. A three-year residency in pediatrics is required. Subspecialization requires further training. Subspecialties of pediatrics include the following fields:

- **Pediatric cardiologist.** This subspecialist provides comprehensive care from fetal life to young adulthood to patients with cardiovascular disorders.
- **Pediatric critical care.** This subspecialist has special competence in advanced life support for children from the newborn to the young adult.
- **Pediatric endocrinologist.** This subspecialist provides expert care to infants, children, and adolescents who have diseases that stem from the glands that secrete hormones.
- **Pediatric hematologist-oncologist.** This subspecialist deals with blood disorders and cancer in infants, children, teens, and young adults.
- **Neonatal-perinatal medicine.** This subspecialist provides care for sick newborns. He or she consults both with obstetrical colleagues in planning care for infants of high-risk pregnancies and with pediatricians on the care of premature babies.
- **Pediatric nephrologist.** This subspecialist deals with the normal and abnormal development of the kidney and urinary tract from fetal life to young adulthood.
- **Pediatric pulmonologist.** This subspecialist deals with the prevention and treatment of respiratory diseases affecting infants, children, and young adults.

Obstetrics and Gynecology

Obstetrics and gynecology (OB/GYN) is a specialty devoted entirely to women. It entails two parts: gynecology, which treats diseases of the female reproductive system, including cancer; and obstetrics, which deals with the care of women before, during, and after they give birth.

Obstetricians/gynecologists have some interesting issues facing them in today's medical environment. Biomedical research has produced profound advances in obstetrical care. These advances have benefited patients, but have also led to higher, and perhaps unrealistic, expectations among patients. The threat of a malpractice suit following a delivery is of such concern that it has led some OB/GYNs to give up the obstetrics part of their practices and practice only gynecology. There is also competition from other professional disciplines that deliver babies, notably family physicians and nurse-midwives.

Another development is the relative maturity of women giving birth for the first time. This reflects trends of the second half of the twentieth century, when more women delayed having children until they were into their thirties or forties. OB/GYN specialists must therefore be equipped to deal with the issues of fertility and childbirth that these patients present.

Most OB/GYN patients are healthy. If they are pregnant, their OB/GYN participates in a very important experience and time in their lives. This is also a specialty with erratic hours, and it makes many demands on its practitioners. Conditions that an OB/GYN might treat other than prenatal care are yeast infections, pelvic pain, endometriosis, infertility, and cancer of the reproductive organs. OB/GYNs are medical doctors and surgeons and enjoy blending both of those aspects of their profession.

OB/GYNs are many women's primary care specialists, and they form close and continuing relationships with their patients. A very small percentage of OB/GYNs include male infertility in their practices. Good manual dexterity is required because this is a hands-on specialty. OB/GYNs divide their time between the office and the hospital.

In 1982, 34 percent of medical school graduates planning to practice OB/GYN were women. By 2002, women made up 72 percent of the 4,656 residents training in 254 accredited programs in OB/GYN.

OB/GYNs have long, erratic hours and very high liability premiums. Their average income ranges from $215,000 to $270,000. In 2002 the average liability premium for self-employed OB/GYNs was $49,530. Premiums in 2003 ranged from a high in Florida of $249,200 to a low of $14,662 in South Dakota.

This specialty requires a four-year residency in obstetrics and gynecology. Subspecialization requires two or three years of further training. Subspecialties of OB/GYN include maternal-fetal medicine, which deals with high-risk patients; reproductive endocrinology, which deals with infertility; and gynecologic oncology, which deals with cancers of the reproductive system.

Anesthesiology

The American Board of Anesthesiology defines anesthesia as a specialty that deals with pain management during and after surgery; cardiac and respiratory resuscitation; application of specific methods of inhalation therapy; and clinical management of various fluid, electrolyte, and metabolic disturbances. Anesthesiologists may also treat cancer pain problems.

In lay terms, the anesthesiologist manages pain during surgical, obstetrical, and some medical procedures and provides life support under the stress of anesthesia and surgery. Anesthesiologists must have a vast knowledge of physiology and pharmacology.

There is a high level of pressure for anesthesiologists because they face calls for quick decision making in life-and-death situations. If they are the only anesthesiologist on call at a busy hospital, they can have long hours in surgery. Anesthesiologists work with a range of health professionals.

Anesthesiologists spend most of their time in hospitals. This is not a specialty that features close, continuing relationships with patients. Most of an anesthesiologist's contact with patients comes presurgically to evaluate the patient, describe the procedure, and help manage anxiety. Their last encounter with the patient is usually right after surgery.

The surgical procedures that they participate in range from the very routine, like tonsillectomies, to the very complicated, like open-heart surgery. This makes their jobs very diverse. They face some competition from nurse anesthesiologists.

The unpredictability of the circumstances makes this a high-pressure field. Income ranges from $242,900 to $334,000 and liability premiums can be high.

In 2002 there were 4,578 residents in 132 accredited training programs for anesthesiologists. Women made up 26 percent of this population. A four-year residency is required for those who specialize in anesthesiology.

Nuclear Medicine

Nuclear medicine is a relatively new specialty. It grew out of the fields of radiology, internal medicine, and pathology. It is mainly a diagnostic discipline. For many years x-rays were the only way to see images inside a person's body. Today there are MRI (magnetic resonance imaging) and PET (positron emission tomography), to name just two new technologies. These approaches to diagnosis are opening new vistas in the study of human disease. The word *nuclear* applied in this way refers to employing the nuclear properties of radioactive and stable nuclides in diagnosis, therapy, and research.

The Joint Commission on the Accreditation of Healthcare Organizations (JCAHO) has stipulated that all hospitals with 300 beds or more should provide nuclear medicine services under the supervision of a qualified nuclear medicine specialist. These procedures are no longer the province only of academic teaching centers. Persons entering this specialty should be prepared for a rapidly evolving field and should thrive on problem solving.

High-tech equipment is at the core of the nuclear physician's specialty. Therefore, very few nuclear physicians are in private practice because the cost of such equipment is prohibitive. Most practice their specialties within the hospital setting. As a result, they are somewhat constrained by the hospital administration's willingness or ability to keep a department of nuclear medicine up-to-date.

It is frequently easier to secure a job after residency with the addition of training in radiology. Patient involvement is often limited, so those desiring long-term relationships with patients will not be satisfied with this field. Common conditions that nuclear physicians encounter include thyroid disease, cardiovascular disease, bone pain, and cancer. Most of their patient encounters are with adults and the elderly.

Specialists in this field have flexible hours and a high level of autonomy. Many enjoy the scientific precision with which they can diagnose an illness. Since they diagnose diseases from across the spectrum, there is a high degree of interaction with physicians from other specialties.

In 2002 there were 115 residents in 65 accredited training programs in nuclear medicine. Women made up 24 percent of residents in nuclear medicine. A minimum of three years of residency training are necessary to qualify for specialty certification. One year should be in an approved medical specialty, followed by two years in a nuclear medicine residency.

Medical Genetics

Medical genetics is a very new medical specialty, and it is one of the most rapidly advancing fields in medicine. Medical genetics is both a basic biomedical science and a clinical specialty. Specialists in this field use their understanding of genetic factors in health and disease to treat patients. Among the issues medical geneticists deal with are the nature of mutations, factors that affect development, and patterns of inherited characteristics. This field looks at genetic diseases like sickle cell anemia and birth defects and probes into how they can be managed. Medical geneticists are very involved in research, as this is a revolutionary new field.

Disease prediction and prevention are at the heart of medical genetics. Medical geneticists have almost eliminated the hereditary Tay-Sachs disease. Because of the emotional aspect of predicting genetic disease, physicians who practice in this specialty need to be very sensitive to their patients' feelings. Also, the novelty of this specialty calls for cutting-edge medical techniques and clinical practices.

In 1997 the Residency Review Committee for the American Council of Graduate Medical Education began accrediting clinical training programs in medical genetics. By 2002 there were 68 residents in 47 accredited training programs. Of these, 57 percent were women. A minimum of four years of residency training are necessary to qualify for specialty certification. Two years must be spent in a residency program in medical genetics. Because of the rapidly evolving nature of this specialty, the requirements for certification are certain to change over the coming years.

Allergy and Immunology

The field of allergy and immunology deals with the human body's reaction to foreign substances. It was officially designated a specialty in 1972 with the formation of the American Board of Allergy and Immunology. Specialists in this profession follow one of two distinct career paths: clinical practice or academic research. This is a rapidly expanding field, with many opportunities for exciting research.

Those in clinical practice treat a range of ages from the very young to the very old. They often develop close, long-term relationships with their patients. The majority of their patients are generally healthy. Practitioners in this specialty have regular hours and a lack of emergency cases.

Allergist/immunologists find that certain other specialties also perform some of their procedures. Depending upon which part of the specialty they practice, practitioners from rheumatology, hematology, otolaryngology, or pulmonology may overlap and create competition for allergist/immunologists.

This specialty sees many positive outcomes and allergist/immunologists can help people suffering from allergic complaints feel much better and lead normal lives. Often entire families have similar patterns of allergies. In this aspect, allergist/immunologists are like family practitioners in that they sometimes treat the whole family. These practitioners spend some of their time with patients teaching them how to manage their allergies. Conditions that these specialists commonly treat are eczema, asthma, chronic cold symptoms, and food and drug allergies.

Even for a physician only involved in clinical practice, this is a diverse field. Because it involves two related but separate disciplines, there is variety in the practice. Annual liability premiums are low. Average income ranges from $91,000 to $181,000.

In 2002 there were 255 residents in 70 accredited programs in allergy and immunology. Women accounted for 49 percent of residents in this specialty. Three years of residency in either internal medicine or pediatrics are required before a residency of at least two years in allergy and immunology.

Dermatology

Dermatology deals with disorders and diseases of the largest organ—the skin. Dermatologists deal with minor skin problems such as warts, acne, and eczema. But they also handle the removal and biopsy of skin tumors, which demands expert diagnostic skill. Dermatologists are called on regularly by other specialists to help figure out complicated diagnoses. Many dermatologists find they prefer either diagnosis or a procedure-oriented practice.

Other conditions that a dermatologist commonly treats are psoriasis, skin cancers, sun damage, and contact dermatitis. Dermatology is a results-oriented profession, and dermatologists have the benefit of seeing fairly quick results. They typically see relatively healthy patients. The noncritical nature of most dermatological problems allows for regular working hours.

Dermatologists spend most of their time in office settings. To diagnose well, dermatologists must have excellent vision. Many diagnoses are made in dermatology on the basis of the way something looks.

Dermatologists have a mix of patient relationships, from short-term to long-term. Urban areas tend to be well saturated with dermatologists. Liability premiums are on the low side, but salaries are fairly high, averaging from $126,000 to $259,000.

In 2002 there were 932 residents in 107 accredited training programs in dermatology. Women accounted for 58 percent of these residents. The American Board of Dermatology requires four years of residency training, including three years of training in dermatology. Subspecialization requires further training. Dermopathology and dermatological immunology/diagnostic laboratory immunology are the two subspecialties of dermatology.

Emergency Medicine

Specialists in emergency medicine are found primarily in hospital emergency departments. Emergency medicine is the medical specialty that calls for the immediate decision making and action necessary to prevent further disability or death. Because they don't have practices, most emergency room physicians aren't responsible for their own liability insurance; it is usually paid for by the hospital. They have very little or no overhead because they don't have offices.

Emergency specialists treat all age groups. They make critical decisions on the spot about a patient's welfare, often without a medical history and sometimes when the patient is unconscious. They must be well versed in an infinite variety of illnesses and disorders. Subspecialties in emergency medicine include undersea and hyperbaric medicine and medical toxicology.

Emergency specialists also must have good interpersonal skills and composure in a fast-paced emergency room. The hours are usually regular because emergency physicians rotate on a schedule. But emergency rooms are staffed all night, and this means emergency physicians often have overnight shifts. Switching back and forth from day to night hours can be difficult. Holidays and weekends must be staffed in an emergency room as well. Although there is ample time off, shifts can cut into valued personal or family time.

This is not a specialty for those desiring long-term, close relationships with patients. Emergency physicians have no control over who their patients are; they must provide care to anyone who comes through the door. It is also important to note that some people use emergency rooms as primary care facilities. Therefore, emergency physicians see a good number of nonemergency situations such as flu, strep throat, and twisted ankles. But depending upon the location of emergency rooms, physicians also see major trauma like gunshot wounds and the results of bad car accidents. Average salaries range from $178,300 to $224,000.

In 2002 there were 3,846 residents in 127 accredited training programs in emergency medicine. Of these, 30 percent were women. An emergency medicine residency is three years long.

Neurology

Neurologists diagnose and treat all types of diseases of the brain, spinal cord, peripheral nerves and muscles, and the nervous system. They work with people who have epilepsy, cerebral palsy, retardation, stroke, Parkinson's disease, muscular dystrophy, multiple sclerosis, Alzheimer's disease, and serious headaches. They use diagnostic tests like EEGs. Neurologists use medication and other noninvasive procedures to treat their patients; neurosurgeons use surgery to treat some of the same illnesses. Neurologists often have long-term relationships with their patients, as most of the diseases they treat are chronic ones. Great strides are being made in the treatment of some diseases such as Parkinson's and stroke, so this work can be very rewarding.

In the subspecialty of pediatric neurology, physicians work with children. Other neurologists may have mostly elderly patients with Alzheimer's and Parkinson's.

Average income for neurologists ranges from $152,000 to $220,900. While this is considerably less than what neurosurgeons earn, liability insurance premiums are much lower for neurologists since their work is less invasive.

Neurology has a four-year residency. In 2002 there were 1,291 residents in 119 accredited training programs for neurologists. About 39 percent of them were women.

Pathology

The medical specialty of pathology deals with the causes, manifestations, and diagnoses of diseases. There are two main ways to practice pathology. One is in a hospital, investigating the effects of disease on the human body. These pathologists perform autopsies and examine tissues removed from patients in biopsies or surgical procedures. This is called anatomical pathology. The other way to practice pathology is as a clinical pathologist. These pathologists work in laboratories supervising testing procedures. Many patients never see the pathologists who help diagnose them.

Also of interest is the exploding technology in pathology. Now more than ever, pathologists can make significant contributions to medicine.

Pathology is a laboratory-oriented discipline, and there is little patient contact. There is, however, considerable contact with other specialists. Pathology is diverse, since it spans all medical specialties. Pathologists have regular hours. There is a need for management skills in pathology because some pathologists run large labs. Average salaries in this field range from $167,000 to $294,500 and liability insurance premiums are low.

In 2002 there were 2,289 residents in 153 accredited programs in pathology. Women accounted for 50 percent of residents in this specialty. The American Board of Pathology offers certification in either anatomic or clinical pathology or both. The combined certification takes five years to complete. Subspecialties of pathology include the following fields:

- **Blood banking.** A physician specializing in blood banking is responsible for the maintenance of an adequate blood supply, blood donor and patient-recipient safety, and appropriate blood utilization. The blood-banking specialist directs the preparation and safe use of specially prepared blood components, including red blood cells, white blood cells, platelets, and plasma constituents.
- **Chemical pathology.** This specialty deals with the biochemistry of the body as it applies to the cause and progress of disease. This specialty includes the application of biochemical data to the detection, confirmation, or monitoring of a disease. The chemical pathologist often serves as a consultant in the diagnosis and treatment of disease.
- **Dermopathology.** This specialty diagnoses and monitors diseases of the skin. The dermopathologist often serves as a clinical consultant and must have in-depth knowledge of dermatology, microbiology, parasitology, new technology, and laboratory management.
- **Forensic pathology.** This specialty investigates cases of sudden, unexpected, suspicious, or violent death as well as other specific classes of death defined by law. The forensic pathologist

sometimes serves the public by becoming a coroner or medical examiner.

• **Hematology/pathology.** This specialty deals with diseases that affect the bone marrow, blood cells, blood clotting mechanisms, and lymph nodes. Hematologists/pathologists function as consultant to all physicians.

• **Immunopathology.** This specialty is concerned with the scientific study of the causes, the diagnosis, and prognosis of disease using the application of immunological principles to the analysis of tissues, cells, and body fluids.

• **Medical microbiology.** The practitioner in medical microbiology isolates and identifies microbial agents that cause infectious diseases. He or she serves as a consultant to primary care physicians when they are dealing with patients with infectious diseases.

• **Neuropathology.** This specialty deals with the diagnoses of diseases of the nervous system and muscles. Neuropathologists often serve as consultants to neurologists and neurosurgeons.

Physical Medicine and Rehabilitation

Physical medicine and rehabilitation, also called *physiatry*, deals with diagnosing, evaluating, and treating patients with impairments and disabilities that involve musculoskeletal, neurologic, cardiovascular, and other body systems. The focus is on the restoration of physical, psychological, social, and vocational function and on alleviation of pain.

Physiatry is a broad field with many opportunities, both in practice and in research. Some physiatrists work in hospital settings helping to restore stroke or accident victims to a functioning life. This type of practice demands knowledge of, and intersects with, many areas of medicine including orthopaedics, neurology, psychiatry, internal medicine, urology, and geriatrics. Other physiatrists have private practices and specialize in areas like sports medicine. In addition, physiatrists also treat arthritis, amputations, back and neck pain, and head and spinal cord trauma.

A high degree of patient and family contact are typical in physiatry. The hours are regular. There is considerable opportunity for patient education, and there can be a great deal of satisfaction inherent in watching the progress that patients make. Average salaries range from $123,000 to $183,000. Liability insurance costs are relatively low.

In 2002 there were 1,097 residents in 80 accredited training programs in physical medicine and rehabilitation. Women made up 35 percent of residents in this specialty. One year of a general internal medicine residency is usually required before a physical medicine and rehabilitation residency of three years can be entered, although some programs offer first-year residencies in this specialty.

Preventive Medicine

Preventive medicine encompasses general preventive medicine, public health, occupational medicine, and aerospace medicine. It requires knowledge and skill in management, epidemiology, health education and health policy, nutrition, biostatistics, and health services administration. Physicians in this field are employed by the armed forces, government, hospitals, and industry.

This is not a specialty that includes a lot of contact with people. Using the preventive frame of reference, the community is the patient, and the physician's focus is on treating the root causes of disease. These causes can include environmental factors, lifestyle, nutrition, or behavior. These specialists are in the public eye because they help make health policy decisions.

An interesting aspect of this specialty is that practitioners often deal with people outside the health arena, such as politicians, lawyers, and economists. There is a community-wide or even global approach to this type of medicine, so the gains that are made have the potential to help thousands or even millions of people. Issues that preventive medicine specialists deal with include sexually transmitted diseases, obesity, cholesterol problems, teen pregnancy, environmental hazards, and smoking. Both AIDS and terrorism have created a need for more government public health workers.

Average salaries in this field range from $80,000 to $183,000 and liability insurance is not usually an issue.

In 2002 there were 333 residents in 83 accredited training programs in general preventive health, occupational health, public health, and aerospace medicine. Women accounted for 40 percent of residents in preventive medicine. One year of clinical training is a prerequisite to entering residency in preventive medicine. Residency typically includes one academic year leading to a master's degree in public health, or equivalent degree, and one year of training in the field. Advanced training may focus on public health, general preventive medicine, occupational medicine, or aerospace medicine. Completion of a residency plus a fourth year of training is required in each of the subspecialties by the American Board of Preventive Medicine.

Psychiatry

Psychiatrists diagnose and treat mental, emotional, and behavioral disorders. Although they have the same medical school training as other physicians, they often use some form of talk therapy as a basis for treatment. This can take the form of individual therapy or group therapy. There have been great advances in understanding the biochemical basis of behavior. As a result, pharmacologic interventions are being used more often to treat mental and emotional problems.

Psychiatry is a profession that calls for strong communication skills. Psychiatrists, more than any other practitioners of medicine, must use all their knowledge to understand the patient's frame of reference. Psychiatry is different from other fields of medicine because at its core it centers on a patient's beliefs, values, and goals.

Psychiatry is an intellectually rigorous and reflective profession. It demands that the practitioner challenge his or her own beliefs regularly. There can be a great deal of satisfaction in seeing patients gain confidence and improve their lives.

However, some patients' conditions are chronic, and the person considering psychiatry must learn to live with the fact that some patients will never get fully well. Some conditions like schizophrenia create long-term problems. Other conditions that psychiatrists treat include depression, anxiety, personality disorders, and chemical and alcohol dependency.

Subspecialties in psychiatry include forensic psychiatry and neurodevelopmental disabilities.

Psychiatrists who are self-employed can set their own hours. Gross annual average income ranges from $131,000 to $164,000. Liability premiums are low. Psychiatrists face competition from other therapists, such as psychologists and social workers. However, generally only psychiatrists can prescribe medication for their patients.

In 2002 there were 4,399 residents in 180 accredited training programs in psychiatry. Of these, 49 percent were women. The American Board of Psychiatry and Neurology requires a broad-based first year of clinical training followed by a three-year residency in psychiatry. Additional training is required for the subspecialties, such as child psychiatry and geriatric psychiatry.

Radiology

Radiology deals with diagnosis and treatment of disease using radium-based substances and instruments. Radiologists formerly were trained in both diagnosis and treatment, but today separate programs exist for each of these aspects of practice.

Radiologists are primarily consultants. The diagnostic radiologists use x-rays and other forms of radiation to assist other physicians in diagnosing disease. Other radiologists use radiation to treat various forms of cancer. Both types of radiology are mostly hospital based. Rapidly expanding technology demands that radiologists constantly update their knowledge to embrace an ever-evolving constellation of diagnostic and treatment techniques.

Although radiologists do have contact with patients, there is little long-term care involved in radiology. Conditions that radiologists commonly deal with are gastrointestinal complaints, cardiovascular disease, cancers, pulmonary disease, trauma, and hypertension. The hours are fairly regular, as radiologists are mostly behind the scenes in medicine. Average annual gross income ranges from $192,000 to $386,000. There is some competition from the field of nuclear medicine.

In 2002 there were 3,906 residents in 193 accredited programs in diagnostic radiology; 26 percent of these were women. There were 503 residents in 79 accredited training programs in radiation oncology; 29 percent of these were women. A four-year residency in diagnostic radiology is required by the American Board of Radiology. The major subspecialties are nuclear radiology and pediatric radiology.

8

MEDICINE IN THE TWENTY-FIRST CENTURY

NEVER BEFORE HAS someone entering the medical profession had so many options. The field of medical practice has expanded beyond the wildest dreams of early practitioners. When a medical school graduate takes the Hippocratic Oath, he or she enters into an occupation with many rewards and many challenges. However, one aspect of the medical profession has remained the same: to be a good doctor, you must truly care about the well-being of your patients. The desire to excel at this profession must be based on the ability to focus, one by one, on the needs of the real people who come seeking your help and guidance in relieving their pain and suffering. This chapter touches on several of the issues and areas of interest in medicine at the beginning of the twenty-first century.

Job Outlook

Due to the expansion of the health care industries, which are expected to grow twice as quickly as the overall economy, employment of physicians will continue to rise during the first decade of this century. In 1970 there were approximately 240,000 physicians practicing in the United States. In 2002 there were more than 583,000 physicians in active practice across the country. About half worked in office-based practices, including clinics and health maintenance organizations (HMOs). Only one in six was self-employed. A quarter of all physicians were employed by hospitals and the rest by federal, state, and local government; educational institutions; and outpatient care centers.

Several organizations, including the National Academy of Sciences Institute of Medicine and the Pew Health Professions Commission, believe that there will be an oversupply of physicians in the years ahead. This is due in part to the increased efficiency and reduced costs demanded by managed care plans such as health maintenance organizations, as care for patients is shifted from physicians to other medical professionals, such as physician assistants and highly skilled nurses.

Although the prediction of oversupply of physicians in some subspecialties such as gastroenterology, medical oncology, and hematology is real, according to the Bureau of Labor Statistics the need for physicians will grow about as fast as the population. An aging population will drive the growth in demand. Also, the employment outlook for physicians will remain strong in rural and low-income areas. These areas are what the U.S. Department of Health and Human Services calls Health Professional Shortage Areas (HPSAs). More than 46 million people live in such areas in the United States,

54 percent of them in inner cities and 46 percent in rural areas. The need for physicians in HPSAs is critical. For example, in these areas children are still dying of diseases such as measles that should have been thoroughly eradicated by vaccination programs. People in the HPSAs also are more likely to suffer from high infant mortality, lead poisoning, tuberculosis, and AIDS.

The changing demographics of the United States have also created a need for physicians who are conversant in other languages and knowledgeable of other cultures. In some large cities, physicians now treat a patient population that speaks dozens of different languages.

Alternative Medicine

Currently, about two in five Americans say that they use alternative therapies when they are sick. The therapies that they seek include homeopathy, nutritional supplements, acupuncture, and meditation. Traditionally, the medical profession has dismissed alternative medicine as essentially voodoo medicine, rooted in superstition and mysticism.

Times have changed. Faced with the fact that many of their patients are employing alternative medical strategies, more than half of the nation's 126 medical schools, including prestigious institutions such as Harvard, Columbia, and Stanford, include some training in alternative medicine. Medical students can now enroll in classes that introduce them to topics such as acupuncture, herbal medicine, and therapeutic massage.

This is not to say that alternative medicine has completely entered the realm of acceptance. Instead, there is a new emphasis on subjecting alternative medicine to the traditional rigors of medical research. In 1998 the alternative medicine office at the National Institutes of Health was transformed into the National Center for Complementary and Alternative Medicine, with a budget of $50 million. This center is involved in studying the effectiveness of alternative treatments.

Patients' Rights

Changes in the way that health care is delivered have changed the face of medicine. Health maintenance organizations and insurance companies sometimes limit the ability of physicians to provide their patients with the care they believe is necessary. Physicians also must now spend more time on paperwork and record keeping. On the other hand, HMOs and increased insurance coverage allow people who may have gone untreated previously to receive medical care.

Nevertheless, there is a sense of increased dissatisfaction within the health care field. The intricacies of health plans often leave doctors and patients confused as to what tests and procedures are covered.

As a response to the growing concerns of patients, the American Medical Association (AMA) has proposed a Patients' Bill of Rights that would be passed by Congress and signed by the President of the United States. This bill of rights would require managed care plans to meet certain standards. The AMA has targeted eight key elements essential to patients' rights legislation. One of these is that decisions regarding "medical necessity" must be made "in a simple, timely process that is fair to the patient, the physician, and the plan." Another proposal is that patients should be allowed to choose their providers and must have access to specialty care where required. The AMA also wants the practice of health plan "gag clauses and gag practices" to be banned. These clauses and practices sometimes prohibit doctors from providing all the available information, tests, and procedures to patients who are covered by restrictive medical plans.

Insurance companies generally oppose such a measure, as they believe it will result in higher medical costs and thus limit the number of people who can be served. The debate over the cost and practice of medicine is likely to continue in the twenty-first century. More than 40 states have passed patient protection legislation.

Conclusion

Modern medicine is undergoing revolutionary changes. Every day there are new discoveries, as physicians and researchers explore the outer limits of medical knowledge. Where medicine was once the domain of the magician, medical professionals are now regarded as scientific experts. The influence of physicians, however, goes beyond curing diseases and repairing broken limbs. They also serve as teachers, providing information to help people live healthier, happier lives. Physicians are perceived as people who serve others, giving of themselves to benefit humankind.

Appendix A

Medical Schools in the United States and Canada

THESE MEDICAL SCHOOLS are accredited by the Liaison Committee on Medical Education of the American Medical Association and the Association of American Medical Colleges. They are listed alphabetically in order of state or province.

Some state universities have campuses offering the first two years of medical training; students then transfer to the main medical campus for the last two years. For example, the University of Minnesota Medical School has a branch campus in Duluth and the University of Illinois Medical School has one in Champaign-Urbana. Because these programs are not accredited independently, they are not listed here.

United States

Alabama

University of Alabama School of Medicine
Office of Medical Student Services/Admissions
1813 Sixth Ave. South
Birmingham, AL 35294
main.uab.edu/uasom

University of South Alabama College of Medicine
Office of Admissions
Medical Sciences Bldg.
307 University Blvd., Rm. 2015
Mobile, AL 36688
southalabama.edu/com

Arizona

University of Arizona College of Medicine
Admissions Office
P.O. Box 245018
Tucson, AZ 85724
medicine.arizona.edu

Arkansas

University of Arkansas College of Medicine
Office of Student Admissions
4301 W. Markham St.
Little Rock, AR 72205
uams.edu/com

California

Loma Linda University School of Medicine
Associate Dean for Admissions
Loma Linda, CA 92350
llu.edu/llu/medicine

Stanford University School of Medicine
Office of Admissions
300 Pasteur Dr., Alway Bldg. M121
Palo Alto, CA 94305
med.stanford.edu

University of California, Davis School of Medicine
Admissions Office
One Shields Ave.
Davis, CA 95616
http://som.ucdavis.edu

University of California, Irvine College of Medicine
Office of Admissions
Medical Education Bldg. 802
Irvine, CA 92697
ucihs.uci.edu/com

University of California, Los Angeles Geffen School of Medicine
Division of Admissions
10823 LeConte Ave.
Los Angeles, CA 90095
medsch.ucla.edu

University of California, San Diego School of Medicine
Office of Admissions
Rm. 162, Medical Teaching Facility
9500 Gilman Dr.
La Jolla, CA 92093
medicine.ucsd.edu

University of California, San Francisco School of Medicine
Office of Admissions
Rm. C-200, Box 0408
San Francisco, CA 94143
http://medsch.ucsf.edu

University of Southern California Keck School of Medicine
Office of Admissions
1975 Zonal Ave., KAM 500
Los Angeles, CA 90033
usc.edu/schools/medicine

Colorado

University of Colorado School of Medicine
Medical School Admissions
4200 E. Ninth Ave., C-297
Denver, CO 80262
uchsc.edu/sm/sm

Connecticut

University of Connecticut School of Medicine
Office of Admissions and Student Affairs
263 Farmington Ave., Rm. AG-062
Farmington, CT 06030
http://medicine.uchc.edu

Yale University School of Medicine
Office of Admissions
333 Cedar St.
New Haven, CT 06510
info.med.yale.edu/ysm

District of Columbia

George Washington University School of Medicine and
 Health Science
Office of Admissions
2300 Eye St. NW
Washington, DC 20037
gwumc.edu/smhs

Georgetown University School of Medicine
Office of Admissions
3900 Reservoir Rd. NW
Washington, DC 20007
http://som.georgetown.edu

Howard University College of Medicine
Admissions Office
520 W St. NW
Washington, DC 20059
med.howard.edu

Florida

Florida State University College of Medicine
Admissions Office
1269 W. Call St.
Tallahassee, FL 32306
med.fsu.edu

University of Florida College of Medicine
Chair, Medical Selection Committee
J. Hillis Miller Health Center
Gainesville, FL 32610
med.ufl.edu

University of Miami School of Medicine
Office of Admissions
P.O. Box 016099
Miami, FL 33101
med.miami.edu

University of South Florida College of Medicine
Office of Admissions
12901 Bruce B. Downs Blvd.
Tampa, FL 33612
med.usf.edu/medicine

Georgia

Emory University School of Medicine
Woodruff Health Sciences Center
Administration Bldg.
1440 Clifton Rd. NE
Atlanta, GA 30322
emory.edu/whsc/med

Medical College of Georgia School of Medicine
Associate Dean for Admissions
1120 Fifteenth St.
Augusta, GA 30912
mcg.edu/som

Mercer University School of Medicine
Office of Admissions and Student Affairs
1550 College St.
Macon, GA 31207
http://medicine.mercer.edu

Morehouse School of Medicine
Admissions and Student Affairs
720 Westview Dr., SW
Atlanta, GA 30310
msm.edu

Hawaii

University of Hawaii, John A. Burns School of Medicine
Office of Admissions
1960 East-West Rd.
Honolulu, HI 96822
http://hawaiimed.hawaii.edu

Illinois

The Chicago Medical School of Rosalind Franklin University
Office of Admissions
3333 Green Bay Rd.
North Chicago, IL 60064
rosalindfranklin.edu

Loyola University Chicago, Stritch School of Medicine
Office of Admissions, Rm. 1752
2160 S. First Ave.
Maywood, IL 60153
meddean.luc.edu

Northwestern University, Feinberg School of Medicine
Associate Dean for Admissions
303 E. Chicago Ave.
Chicago, IL 60611
medschool.northwestern.edu

Rush Medical College of Rush University
Office of Admissions
600 S. Paulina St.
Chicago, IL 60612
rushu.rush.edu/medcol

Southern Illinois University School of Medicine
Office of Student and Alumni Affairs
P.O. Box 19620
Springfield, IL 62794
siumed.edu

University of Chicago, Pritzker School of Medicine
Office of the Dean of Students
5841 S. Maryland Ave.
Chicago, IL 60637
http://pritzker.bsd.uchicago.edu

University of Illinois, Chicago College of Medicine
Office of Medical College Admissions
Rm. 165 CME M/C 783
1853 W. Polk St.
Chicago, IL 60612
uic.edu/depts/mcam

Indiana

Indiana University School of Medicine
Medical School Admissions Office
1120 South Dr.
Indianapolis, IN 46202
medicine.iu.edu

Iowa

University of Iowa Carver College of Medicine
Director of Admissions
200 Medicine Administration Bldg.
Iowa City, IA 52242
medicine.uiowa.edu

Kansas

University of Kansas School of Medicine
Associate Dean for Admissions
3901 Rainbow Blvd.
Kansas City, KS 66160
kumc.edu/som

Kentucky

University of Kentucky College of Medicine
Admissions Office
Chandler Medical Center
800 Rose St.
Lexington, KY 40536
mc.uky.edu/medicine

University of Louisville School of Medicine
Office of Admissions
Abell Administration Center
323 E. Chestnut St.
Louisville, KY 40202
louisville.edu/medschool

Louisiana

Louisiana State University School of Medicine in New Orleans
Admissions Office
533 Bolivar St.
New Orleans, LA 70112
medschool.lsuhsc.edu

Louisiana State University School of Medicine in Shreveport
Office of Student Admissions
P.O. Box 33932
Shreveport, LA 71130
sh.lsuhsc.edu

Tulane University School of Medicine
Office of Admissions
1430 Tulane Ave.
New Orleans, LA 70112
som.tulane.edu

Maryland

Johns Hopkins University School of Medicine
Committee on Admission
720 Rutland Ave.
Baltimore, MD 21205
hopkinsmedicine.org/som

Uniformed Services University of the Health Sciences,
F. Edward Hebert School of Medicine
Admissions Office, Rm. A-1041
4301 Jones Bridge Rd.
Bethesda, MD 20814
usuhs.mil/medschool/fehsom.html

University of Maryland School of Medicine
Committee on Admissions
655 W. Baltimore St., Rm. 1-005
Baltimore, MD 21201
medschool.umaryland.edu

Massachusetts

Boston University School of Medicine
Admissions Office L-124
715 Albany St.
Boston, MA 02118
bumc.bu.edu/busm

Harvard Medical School
Office of Admissions
25 Shattuck St.
Boston, MA 02115
hms.harvard.edu

Tufts University School of Medicine
Committee on Admissions
136 Harrison Ave.
Boston, MA 02111
tufts.edu/med

University of Massachusetts Medical School
Associate Dean for Admissions
55 Lake Ave. N
Worcester, MA 01655
umassmed.edu

Michigan

Michigan State University College of Human Medicine
Office of Admissions
A-110 E. Fee Hall
East Lansing, MI 48824
chm.msu.edu

University of Michigan Medical School
Admissions Office
1301 Catherine Rd.
Ann Arbor, MI 48109
med.umich.edu/medschool

Wayne State University School of Medicine
Director of Admissions
540 E. Canfield Ave.
Detroit, MI 48201
med.wayne.edu

Minnesota

Mayo Medical School
Admissions Committee
200 First St. SW
Rochester, MN 55905
mayo.edu/mms

University of Minnesota, Twin Cities Medical School
Office of Admissions and Student Affairs
Box 293-UMHC
420 Delaware St. SE
Minneapolis, MN 55455
med.umn.edu
(See http://penguin.d.umn.edu for the Duluth campus.)

Mississippi

University of Mississippi School of Medicine
Chair, Admissions Committee
2500 N. State St.
Jackson, MS 39216
http://som.umc.edu

Missouri

Saint Louis University School of Medicine
Admissions Committee
1402 S. Grand Blvd.
St. Louis, MO 63104
slu.edu/colleges/med

University of Missouri, Columbia School of Medicine
Office of Admissions
MA202 Medical Sciences Bldg.
One Hospital Dr.
Columbia, MO 65212
hsc.missouri.edu/~medicine

University of Missouri, Kansas City School of Medicine
Council on Selection
2411 Holmes
Kansas City, MO 64108
http://research.med.umkc.edu

Washington University School of Medicine
Admissions Office
660 S. Euclid Ave.
P.O. Box 8106
St. Louis, MO 63110
http://medinfo.wustl.edu

Nebraska

Creighton University School of Medicine
Office of Admissions
2500 California Plaza
Omaha, NE 68178
http://medicine.creighton.edu

University of Nebraska College of Medicine
Office of the Dean-Admissions
986545 Nebraska Medical Center
Omaha, NE 68198
unmc.edu/uncom

Nevada

University of Nevada School of Medicine
Office of Admissions and Student Affairs
Savitt Medical Bldg./332
Reno, NV 89557
unr.edu/med

New Hampshire

Dartmouth Medical School
Office of Admissions
3 Rope Ferry Rd.
Hanover, NH 03755
dartmouth.edu/dms

New Jersey

University of Medicine and Dentistry of New Jersey
New Jersey Medical School
Director of Admissions
185 S. Orange Ave.
Newark, NJ 07103
njms.umdnj.edu

University of Medicine and Dentistry of New Jersey
Robert Wood Johnson Medical School
Office of Admissions
675 Hoes La.
Piscataway, NJ 08854
rwjms.umdnj.edu

New Mexico

University of New Mexico School of Medicine
Office of Admissions and Student Affairs
Basic Medical Sciences Bldg., Rm. 107
Albuquerque, NM 87131
http://hsc.unm.edu/som

New York

Albany Medical College
Office of Admissions
47 New Scotland Ave.
Mail Code 34, Rm. MS-129
Albany, NY 12208
amc.edu/academic

Columbia University College of Physicians and Surgeons
Admissions Office
630 W. 168th St., Rm. 1-416
New York, NY 10032
http://cpmcnet.columbia.edu/dept/ps

Cornell University, Weill Medical College
Office of Admissions
1300 York Ave.
New York, NY 10021
med.cornell.edu

Mount Sinai School of Medicine of New York University
Office for Admissions
Annenberg Bldg., Rm. 5-04
One Gustave L. Levy Pl.
New York, NY 10029
mssm.edu

New York Medical College
Office of Admissions
Rm. 127, Sunshine Cottage
Valhalla, NY 10595
nymc.edu

New York University School of Medicine
Office of Admissions
550 First Ave.
New York, NY 10016
med.nyu.edu

State University of New York at Buffalo, School of Medicine and
   Biomedical Sciences
Office of Medical Admissions
3435 Main St.
Buffalo, NY 14214
smbs.buffalo.edu

State University of New York Downstate College of Medicine
Director of Admissions
450 Clarkson Ave., Box 97
Brooklyn, NY 11203
downstate.edu/college_of_medicine

State University of New York Upstate Medical University
   College of Medicine
Admissions Committee
750 Adams St.
Syracuse, NY 13210
upstate.edu

Stony Brook University Health Sciences Center School of Medicine
Committee on Admissions
Level 4, Rm. 169
Stony Brook, NY 11794
hsc.stonybrook.edu/som

University of Rochester School of Medicine and Dentistry
Director of Admissions
601 Elmwood Ave., Box 706
Rochester, NY 14642
urmc.rochester.edu/smd

Yeshiva University, Albert Einstein College of Medicine
Office of Admissions
Jack and Pearl Resnick Campus
1300 Morris Park Ave.
Bronx, NY 10461
aecom.yu.edu

North Carolina

Duke University School of Medicine
Committee on Admissions
P.O. Box 3701
Durham, NC 27710
http://medschool.duke.edu

East Carolina University Brody School of Medicine
Office of Admissions
Greenville, NC 27858
ecu.edu/med

University of North Carolina at Chapel Hill School of Medicine
Admissions Office
CB# 9500, Rm. 121 MacNider Hall
Chapel Hill, NC 27599
med.unc.edu

Wake Forest University School of Medicine
Office of Medical School Admissions
Medical Center Blvd.
Winston-Salem, NC 27157
wfubmc.edu

North Dakota

University of North Dakota School of Medicine and
    Health Sciences
Committee on Admissions
501 N. Columbia Rd., Box 9037
Grand Forks, ND 58202
med.und.nodak.edu

Ohio

Case Western Reserve University School of Medicine
Associate Dean for Admissions and Student Affairs
10900 Euclid Ave.
Cleveland, OH 44106
http://mediswww.meds.cwru.edu

Medical College of Ohio
Admissions Office
P.O. Box 10008
Toledo, OH 43699
mco.edu/smed

Northeastern Ohio Universities College of Medicine
Office of Admissions
P.O. Box 95
Rootstown, OH 44272
neoucom.edu

Ohio State University College of Medicine and Public Health
Admissions Committee
254 Meiling Hall
370 W. Ninth Ave.
Columbus, OH 43210
med.ohio-state.edu

University of Cincinnati College of Medicine
Office of Student Affairs/Admissions
P.O. Box 670555
Cincinnati, OH 45267
med.uc.edu

Wright State University School of Medicine
Office of Student Affairs/Admissions
P.O. Box 927
Dayton, OH 45401
med.wright.edu

Oklahoma

University of Oklahoma College of Medicine
P.O. Box 26901
Oklahoma City, OK 73190
medicine.ouhsc.edu

Oregon

Oregon Health and Science University School of Medicine
Office of Education and Student Affairs, L102
3181 S.W. Sam Jackson Park Rd.
Portland, OR 97201
ohsu.edu/som

Pennsylvania

Drexel University College of Medicine
Admissions Office
2900 W. Queen La.
Philadelphia, PA 19129
drexel.edu/med

Jefferson Medical College of Thomas Jefferson University
Associate Dean for Admissions
1025 Walnut St.
Philadelphia, PA 19107
jefferson.edu/jmc

Pennsylvania State University College of Medicine
Office of Student Affairs
P.O. Box 850
Hershey, PA 17033
hmc.psu.edu/college

Temple University School of Medicine
Admissions Office
3400 N. Broad St.
Philadelphia, PA 19140
medschool.temple.edu

University of Pennsylvania School of Medicine
Director of Admissions and Financial Aid
3620 Hamilton Walk
Philadelphia, PA 19104
med.upenn.edu

University of Pittsburgh School of Medicine
Office of Admissions
M240 Scaife Hall
Pittsburgh, PA 15261
medschool.pitt.edu

Puerto Rico

Ponce School of Medicine
Admissions Office
P.O. Box 7004
Ponce, PR 00732
psm.edu

Universidad Central del Caribe School of Medicine
Office of Admissions
Call Box 60-327
Bayamon, PR 00960
uccaribe.edu

University of Puerto Rico School of Medicine
Central Admissions Office
Medical Sciences Campus
P.O. Box 365067
San Juan, PR 00936
rcm.upr.edu

Rhode Island

Brown Medical School
Office of Admissions and Financial Aid
97 Waterman St., Box G-A212
Providence, RI 02912
http://bms.brown.edu

South Carolina

Medical University of South Carolina College of Medicine
Office of Enrollment Services
P.O. Box 250617
Charleston, SC 29425
musc.edu

University of South Carolina School of Medicine
Associate Dean for Student Programs
Columbia, SC 29208
med.sc.edu

South Dakota

University of South Dakota School of Medicine
Office of Student Affairs, Rm. 105
1400 W. Twenty-Second St.
Vermillion, SD 57105
http://med.usd.edu

Tennessee

East Tennessee State University, Quillen College of Medicine
Assistant Dean for Admissions and Records
P.O. Box 70694
Johnson City, TN 37614
http://com.etsu.edu

Meharry Medical College School of Medicine
Director, Admissions and Records
1005 D. B. Todd, Jr. Blvd.
Nashville, TN 37208
mmc.edu

University of Tennessee Health Science Center College of Medicine
Director of Admissions
800 Madison Ave.
Memphis, TN 38163
utmem.edu/medicine

Vanderbilt University School of Medicine
Office of Admissions
Twenty-First Ave., South at Garland Ave.
Nashville, TN 37232
mc.vanderbilt.edu/medschool

Texas

Baylor College of Medicine
Office of Admissions
One Baylor Plaza
Houston, TX 77030
bcm.edu

Texas A&M University System Health Science Center
    College of Medicine
Associate Dean for Admissions and Student Affairs
1114 TAMU
College Station, TX 77843
http://medicine.tamu.edu

Texas Tech University Health Sciences Center School of Medicine
Office of Admissions
Health Sciences Center
3601 Fourth St.
Lubbock, TX 79430
ttuhsc.edu/som

University of Texas Health Science Center at Houston
   Medical School
Office of Admissions
6431 Fannin St., Rm. G-024
Houston, TX 77030
med.uth.tmc.edu

University of Texas Medical Branch at Galveston
Office of Admissions
301 University Blvd.
Galveston, TX 77555
utmb.edu

University of Texas Medical School at San Antonio
Medical School Admissions
7703 Floyd Curl Dr.
San Antonio, TX 78229
http://som.uthscsa.edu

University of Texas Southwestern Medical Center at Dallas
   Southwestern Medical School
Office of the Registrar
5323 Harry Hines Blvd.
Dallas, TX 75390
http://www8.utsouthwestern.edu/home/education/medicalschool

Utah

University of Utah School of Medicine
Director, Medical School Admissions
50 N. Medical Dr.
Salt Lake City, UT 84132
med.utah.edu/som

Vermont

University of Vermont College of Medicine
Admissions Office
E-109 Given Bldg.
Burlington, VT 05405
med.uvm.edu

Virginia

Eastern Virginia Medical School of the Medical College of
   Hampton Roads
Office of Admissions
P.O. Box 1980
Norfolk, VA 23501
www.evms.edu

University of Virginia School of Medicine
Admissions Office
P.O. Box 800793, McKim Hall
Charlottesville, VA 22908
healthsystem.virginia.edu/education-research

Virginia Commonwealth University School of Medicine
Medical School Admissions
P.O. Box 980565
Richmond, VA 23298
medschool.vcu.edu

Washington

University of Washington School of Medicine
Admissions Office
Health Sciences Center A-300, Box 356340
Seattle, WA 98195
uwmedicine.org/education/mdprogram

West Virginia

Marshall University Edwards School of Medicine
Admissions Office
1600 Medical Center Dr.
Huntington, WV 25701
musom.marshall.edu

West Virginia University School of Medicine
Office of Admissions and Records
Health Sciences Center
P.O. Box 9000
Morgantown, WV 26506
hsc.wvu.edu/som

Wisconsin

Medical College of Wisconsin
Office of Admissions and Registrar
8701 Watertown Plank Rd.
Milwaukee, WI 53226
mcw.edu

University of Wisconsin Medical School
Admissions Committee
Medical Sciences Center, Rm. 1250
1300 University Ave.
Madison, WI 53706
med.wisc.edu

Canada

Alberta

University of Alberta Faculty of Medicine and Dentistry
Admissions Officer
252 Mackenzie Health Sciences Centre
Edmonton, AB, Canada T6G 2R7
med.ualberta.ca

University of Calgary Faculty of Medicine
Office of Admissions
3330 Hospital Dr. NW
Calgary, AB, Canada T2N 4N1
med.ucalgary.ca

British Columbia

University of British Columbia Faculty of Medicine
Admissions Office
317-2194 Health Sciences Mall
Vancouver, BC, Canada V6T 1Z3
med.ubc.ca

Manitoba

University of Manitoba Faculty of Medicine
Chair, Admissions Committee
753 McDermot Ave.
Winnipeg, MB, Canada R3E 0W3
umanitoba.ca/faculties/medicine

Newfoundland

Memorial University of Newfoundland Faculty of Medicine
Chair, Committee on Admissions
Health Sciences Centre
St. John's, NF, Canada A1B 3V6
med.mun.ca/med

Nova Scotia

Dalhousie University Faculty of Medicine
Admissions Coordinator
Clinical Research Centre
5849 University Ave.
Halifax, NS, Canada B3H 4H7
medicine.dal.ca

Ontario

McMaster University School of Medicine
Admissions and Records
Rm. IB7-Health Sciences Center
1200 Main St. West
Hamilton, ON, Canada L8N 3Z5
fhs.mcmaster.ca

Queen's University Faculty of Health Sciences School of Medicine
Admissions Office
Kingston, ON, Canada K7L 3N6
http://meds.queensu.ca

University of Ottawa Faculty of Medicine
Admissions
451 Smyth Rd.
Ottawa, ON, Canada K1H 8M5
uottawa.ca/academic/med

University of Toronto Faculty of Medicine
Admissions Office
1 King's College Circle
Toronto, ON, Canada M5S 1A8
facmed.utoronto.ca

University of Western Ontario Faculty of Medicine and Dentistry
Admissions Office
Health Sciences Center, Rm. H-110
London, ON, Canada N6A 5C1
med.uwo.ca

Quebec

McGill University Faculty of Medicine
Admissions Office
3655 Promenade Sir William Osler
Montreal, QC, Canada H3G 1Y6
med.mcgill.ca

University Laval Faculty of Medicine
Admission Committee
Quebec City, QC, Canada G1K 7P4
fmed.ulaval.ca

University of Montreal School of Medicine
Committee on Admission
P.O. Box 6128, Station Centre-Ville
Montreal, QC, Canada H3C 3J7
http://medes3.med.umontreal.ca

University of Sherbrooke Faculty of Medicine
Admission Office
3001 Twelfth Ave. North
Sherbrooke, QC, Canada J1H 5N4
usherbrooke.ca/medecine

Saskatchewan

University of Saskatchewan College of Medicine
Admissions
B 103 Health Sciences Bldg.
Saskatoon, SK, Canada S7N 5E5
usask.ca/medicine

Appendix B

Combined Degree Programs

THE FOLLOWING IS a list of medical schools that, in collaboration with their undergraduate division, accept high school seniors or undergraduates who have completed one or two years of study. In some cases, study toward the M.D. may be completed in fewer than eight years.

The list is organized alphabetically by state, providing the school name, address, and website.

The Association of American Medical Colleges' annual publication *Medical School Admission Requirements* provides detailed descriptions of the programs that combine the baccalaureate degree with an M.D. degree.

Alabama

University of Alabama
Early Medical School Acceptance Program
HUC 260, 1530 Third Ave. South
Birmingham, AL 35294
uab.edu/emsap

University of South Alabama
Office of Admissions
Administrative Bldg., Rm. 182
Mobile, AL 36688
southalabama.edu

California

University of California, San Diego School of Medicine
Medical Scholars Program
Office of Admissions
9500 Gilman Dr.
La Jolla, CA 92093
http://medschool.ucsd.edu/admissions/med_scholar.html
(state residents only)

University of Southern California Keck School of Medicine
College of Letters, Arts, and Sciences
University of Southern California
CAS 100, University Park
Los Angeles, CA 90089
usc.edu/school/medicine/education/degrees_programs/mdp/
    bamd.html

Connecticut

University of Connecticut School of Medicine
Special Program in Medicine
University of Connecticut
2131 Hillside Rd., U-88
Storrs, CT 06269
http://medicine.uchc.edu/departments/studentservices/admissions/
    ba_bs/index.shtml

District of Columbia

George Washington University School of Medicine and
   Columbian College
Office of Admissions
George Washington University
2121 "I" St. NW
Washington, DC 20052
gwired.gwu.edu/adm

Howard University
Center for Preprofessional Education
P.O. Box 473
Administration Bldg.
Washington, DC 20059
med.howard.edu

Florida

University of Florida Junior Honors Medical Program
Admissions Coordinator
P.O. Box 100216
Gainesville, FL 32610
med.ufl.edu/oea/admiss
(state residents only)

University of Miami Honors Program in Medicine
Office of Admissions
P.O. Box 248025
Coral Gables, FL 33124
miami.edu/medical-admissions

University of South Florida
   College of Medicine
   Accelerated Medical School Program
Undergraduate Admissions
4202 E. Fowler Ave., SUC 1036
Tampa, FL 33620
http://hsc.usf.edu/OCME/programs/index.html
(state residents only)

Illinois

Northwestern University Honors Program in Medical Education
Office of Admission and Financial Aid
1801 Hinman Ave.
Evanston, IL 60204
feinberg.northwestern.edu/hpme

University of Illinois at Chicago Guaranteed Professional
   Programs Admissions
P.O. Box 6020
Chicago, IL 60680
uic.edu
(state residents only)

Massachusetts

Boston University
Office of Admissions
121 Bay State Rd.
Boston, MA 02215
bu.edu/discover/medical.html

Michigan

Michigan State University, Advanced Baccalaureate
    Learning Experience
College of Human Medicine
Office of Admissions
A-239 Life Sciences
East Lansing, MI 48824
chm.msu.edu

Wayne State University Honors Program
2100 Undergraduate Library
Detroit, MI 48202
admissions.wayne.edu
(Michigan and western Ohio residents only)

Missouri

Saint Louis University, Preprofessional Health Studies
3840 Lindell Blvd., Ste. 210
Saint Louis, MO 63108
slu.edu/colleges/as/phs/scholars1.html

University of Missouri, Columbia Conley Scholars Program
MA 215 Medical Sciences Bldg.
Columbia, MO 65212
muhealth.edu/medicine
(Missouri and contiguous states residents only)

University of Missouri, Kansas City Six-Year Program
School of Medicine
Council on Selection
2411 Holmes
Kansas City, MO 64108
umkc.edu/medicine

New York

New York University, Prehealth Office
Admissions Office, College of Arts & Science
22 Washington Square North
Rm. 904 Main Bldg.
New York, NY 10011
nyu.edu/ugadmissions

Stony Brook University Scholars for Medicine
Honors College
Stony Brook University
N3070 Melville Library
Stony Brook, NY 11794
stonybrook.edu/honors

University of Rochester
Program Coordinator
Rochester Early Medical Scholars
P.O. Box 270251
Rochester, NY 14627
rochester.edu/admissions/academics/opportunities/#rems

Ohio

Case Western Reserve University, Preprofessional Scholars Program
   in Medicine
Office of Undergraduate Admission
10900 Euclid Ave.
Cleveland, OH 44106
http://admission.case.edu/admissions/academics/ppsp.asp

Ohio State University College of Medicine and Public Health
Early Admission Pathway
209 Meiling Hall
370 W. Ninth Ave.
Columbus, OH 43210
http://medicine.osu.edu/futurestudents/eap.cfm
(National Merit, National Achievement, or National Hispanic
   Scholars finalists only)

Rhode Island

Brown University
Program in Liberal Medical Education Office
P.O. Box 1876
Providence, RI 02912
http://bms.brown.edu/plme

Tennessee

East Tennessee State University
Director, Premedical-Medical Program
Office of Medical Professions Advisement
P.O. Box 70,592
Johnson City, TN 37614
etsu.edu/cas/premed/mpa.htm

Texas

University of Texas Medical School at San Antonio
Admissions Office
7703 Floyd Curl Dr.
San Antonio, TX 78229
http://som.uthscsa.edu
(state residents only)

Wisconsin

University of Wisconsin Medical Scholars Program
1300 University Ave., Rm. 1110
Madison, WI 53706
med.wisc.edu/education/med_scholars/index.php
(state residents only)

The following medical schools accept high school seniors or undergraduates in collaboration with the undergraduate divisions of affiliated institutions. The list is organized alphabetically by state and gives the medical school (MD) as well as the affiliated undergraduate institution or institutions (UG). In most cases, application is first made to the undergraduate school.

California

University of California, Los Angeles Geffen School of
    Medicine (MD)
University of California, Riverside (UG)
Thomas Haider Program in Biomedical Sciences
Student Affairs Officer
Division of Biomedical Sciences
University of California, Riverside
Riverside, CA 92521
biomed.ucr.edu

Illinois

The Chicago Medical School of Rosalind Franklin University (MD)
Illinois Institute of Technology (UG)
Director of Admissions
B.S./M.D. Program
Illinois Institute of Technology
10 W. Thirty-Third St.
Chicago, IL 60616
iit.edu/~epremed

Massachusetts

Tufts University School of Medicine (MD)
Tufts University, Boston College, Brandeis University (UG)
Admissions Office
Tufts University
715 Albany St.
Boston, MA 02118
tufts.edu/med/admissions/program_ba_med.html

New Jersey

UMDNJ-New Jersey Medical School (MD)
Boston University, Drew University, Montclair State University,
　New Jersey Institute of Technology, Rutgers University-Newark,
　Stevens Institute of Technology, Richard Stockton College of
　New Jersey, The College of New Jersey (UG)
Office of Admissions
New Jersey Medical School
C-653 MSB
185 S. Orange Ave.
Newark, NJ 07101
njms.umdnj.edu

UMDNJ-Robert Wood Johnson Medical School (MD)
Rutgers University (UG)
Bachelor/Medical Degree Program
Nelson Biological Laboratory
Rutgers University
604 Allison Rd.
Piscataway, NJ 08854
lifesci.rutgers.edu/~hpo

New York

Albany Medical College (MD)
Rensselaer Polytechnic Institute Physician-Scientist Program, Siena
　College, Union College-Leadership in Medicine Program (UG)
Albany Medical College
Office of Admissions
47 New Scotland Rd.
Albany, NY 12208
amc.edu/academic

SUNY Downstate College of Medicine (MD)
Brooklyn College (UG)
B.A./M.D. Honors Program
Director of Admissions
Brooklyn College
2231 Boylan Hall, 2900 Bedford Ave.
Brooklyn, NY 11210
http://depthome.brooklyn.cuny.edu/bamd/bamdmain.html

SUNY Upstate Medical University (MD)
Wilkes University (UG)
Admissions
Wilkes University
P.O. Box 111
Wilkes-Barre, PA 18766
wilkes.edu
(New York state residents only)

Ohio

Northeastern Ohio Universities College of Medicine (MD)
Kent State University, University of Akron, Youngstown State
    University (UG)
Associate Director of Admissions
Northeastern Ohio Universities College of Medicine
4209 State Route 44, P.O. Box 95
Rootstown, OH 44272
neoucom.edu

University of Cincinnati (MD)

University of Cincinnati, University of Dayton, John Carroll
    University, Miami University, Xavier University (UG)

Dual Admissions Program

University of Cincinnati

231 Albert Sabin Way, Rm. E-251

Cincinnati, OH 45267

med.uc.edu/hs2md

Pennsylvania

Drexel University College of Medicine (MD)

Drexel University, Lehigh University, Villanova University (UG)

Admissions Office

Drexel University College of Medicine

2900 W. Queen La.

Philadelphia, PA 19129

drexel.edu/med

Jefferson Medical College (MD)-Penn State Accelerated Program

Pennsylvania State University (UG)

Undergraduate Admissions

Pennsylvania State University

201 Shields Bldg., Box 3000

University Park, PA 16804

science.psu.edu/academic/premedmed.html

Temple University School of Medicine (MD)
Temple University, Duquesne University, University of Scranton,
   Washington and Jefferson College, Widener University (UG)
Temple University
3400 N. Broad St.
Philadelphia, PA 19140
medschool.temple.edu/admissions/baccalaureate_md.html

Tennessee

Meharry Medical College (MD)
Fisk University (UG)
1000 Seventeenth Ave. North
Nashville, TN 37208
fisk.edu

Texas

Baylor College of Medicine (MD)
Rice University (UG)
Office of Admissions
P.O. Box 1892
Houston, TX 77251
rice.edu

Virginia

Eastern Virginia Medical School (MD)

The College of William and Mary, Old Dominion University, Hampton University, Hampden-Sydney College, Norfolk State University, Virginia Wesleyan College (UG)

Office of Admissions

Eastern Virginia Medical School

721 Fairfax Ave.

Norfolk, VA 23507

evms.edu

Appendix C

Specialty Boards

These boards certify doctors who have completed the appropriate residency in the field. They are all members of the American Board of Medical Specialties (abms.org).

Allergy and Immunology

American Board of Allergy and Immunology
510 Walnut St., Ste. 1701
Philadelphia, PA 19106
abai.org

Anesthesiology

American Board of Anesthesiology
4101 Lake Boone Trail
Raleigh, NC 27607
abanes.org

Colon and Rectal Surgery

American Board of Colon and Rectal Surgery
20600 Eureka Rd., Ste. 600
Taylor, MI 48180
abcrs.org

Dermatology

American Board of Dermatology
Henry Ford Health System
One Ford Place
Detroit, MI 48202
abderm.org

Emergency Medicine

American Board of Emergency Medicine
3000 Coolidge Rd.
East Lansing, MI 48823
abem.org

Family Practice

American Board of Family Practice
2228 Young Dr.
Lexington, KY 40505
abfp.org

Internal Medicine

American Board of Internal Medicine
510 Walnut St., Ste. 1700
Philadelphia, PA 19106
abim.org

Medical Genetics

American Board of Medical Genetics
9650 Rockville Pike
Bethesda, MD 20814
abmg.org

Neurological Surgery

American Board of Neurological Surgery
6550 Fannin St., Ste. 2139
Houston, TX 77030
abns.org

Nuclear Medicine

American Board of Nuclear Medicine
900 Veteran Ave., Rm. 13-152
Los Angeles, CA 90024
abnm.org

Obstetrics and Gynecology

American Board of Obstetrics and Gynecology
2915 Vine St., Ste. 300
Dallas, TX 75204
abog.org

Ophthalmology

American Board of Ophthalmology
111 Presidential Blvd., Ste. 241
Bala Cynwyd, PA 19004
abop.org

Orthopaedic Surgery

American Board of Orthopaedic Surgery
400 Silver Cedar Court
Chapel Hill, NC 27514
abos.org

Otolaryngology

American Board of Otolaryngology
3050 Post Oak Blvd., Ste. 1700
Houston, TX 77056
aboto.org

Pathology

American Board of Pathology
P.O. Box 25915
Tampa, FL 33622-5915
abpath.org

Pediatrics

American Board of Pediatrics
111 Silver Cedar Court
Chapel Hill, NC 27514
abp.org

Physical Medicine and Rehabilitation

American Board of Physical Medicine and Rehabilitation
3-15 Allegro Park La. SW
Rochester, MN 55902
abpmr.org

Plastic Surgery

American Board of Plastic Surgery
Seven Penn Center, Ste. 400
1635 Market St.
Philadelphia, PA 19103
abplsurg.org

Preventive Medicine

American Board of Preventive Medicine
330 S. Wells St., Ste. 1018
Chicago, IL 60606
abprevmed.org

Psychiatry and Neurology

American Board of Psychiatry and Neurology
500 Lake Cook Rd., #335
Deerfield, IL 60015
abpn.com

Radiology

American Board of Radiology
5441 E. Williams Circle, Ste. 200
Tucson, AZ 85711
theabr.org

Surgery

American Board of Surgery
1617 John F. Kennedy Blvd., Ste. 860
Philadelphia, PA 19103
absurgery.org

Thoracic Surgery

American Board of Thoracic Surgery
633 N. St. Clair St., Ste. 2320
Chicago, IL 60611
abts.org

Urology

American Board of Urology
2216 Ivy Rd., Ste. 210
Charlottesville, VA 22903
abu.org

About the Author

Jan Sugar-Webb, M.A., is an award-winning communications and marketing consultant in Chicago. Through her communications firm, Sugar-Webb & Associates, she frequently works with health care organizations and physicians. She is the former director of public affairs at Mount Sinai Hospital on Chicago's west side. Prior to that appointment, she was a research and policy writer for the American Medical Association, where she worked on the *Health Policy Agenda for the American People*, the AMA's blueprint for the delivery of health care in the twenty-first century.

Ms. Sugar-Webb holds a baccalaureate degree in literature from Simmons College in Boston and a master's degree in education from Boston University. Her broad experience as a teacher includes directing a program for high school dropouts from the inner city and implementing a training program for teachers of the disabled at City Colleges of Chicago.